Suffolk County

You may keep th

GW00336767

30127 04980093 6

ETHNIC CLEAVAGES AND CONFLICT: THE SOURCES OF NATIONAL COHESION AND DISINTEGRATION

For my sons, Milosh and Ivan

Ethnic Cleavages and Conflict: The Sources of National Cohesion and Disintegration

The case of Yugoslavia

DR GOJKO VUCKOVIC
Center for Multiethnic and Transnational Studies
University of Southern California, Los Angeles

Ashgate

Aldershot • Brookfield USA • Singapore • Sydney

© Gojko Vuckovic 1997

All rights reserved. No part of this publication may be reproduced, stored in a
retrieval system, or transmitted in any form or by any means, electronic,
mechanical, photocopying, recording or otherwise without the prior permission
of the publisher.

Published by
Ashgate Publishing Ltd
Gower House
Croft Road
Aldershot
Hants GU11 3HR
England

Ashgate Publishing Company
Old Post Road
Brookfield
Vermont 05036
USA

Suffolk County Council
Libraries & Heritage

BFS   7|97

305.8009
4971   L I

British Library Cataloguing in Publication Data

Vuckovic, Gojko
    Ethnic cleavages and conflict : the sources of national
    cohesion and disintegration : the case of Yugoslavia
    3.Yugoslavia - Ethnic relations 4.Yugoslavia - Politics and
    government - 1992-
    I.Title
    305.8'0094971

Library of Congress Catalog Card Number: 97-70896

ISBN 1 85972 640 2

Printed and bound by Athenaeum Press, Ltd.,
Gateshead, Tyne & Wear.

Contents

Maps and tables

Acknowledgements

Writing a book is a lonely scholarship process as well as a lengthy adventure in questioning the existing knowledge and theories about the phenomena humankind are facing today. Full commitment, motivation, and intellectual and physical strength are preconditions for success. In addition, such an adventure is possible to achieve only if one finds love and support from his family. I found it in my family. The love of my sons, Milosh and Ivan, and my wife, Ivana, made the venture of writing this book possible. The love and strength I got from my parents, Milos and Zorka, and my brother, Vladimir, were essential in my scholarship endeavors.

The academic environment I found at the University of Southern California, Los Angeles, contributed the most to finding and addressing the right questions for my book. I am particularly indebted to Professor Catherine Burke, Professor Gerald E. Caiden, Professor Chester Newland, and Professor Steven Lamy for their suggestions and encouragement. My special thanks go to the Dean and Professor of the School of Public Administration, Jane Pisano, and Professor Peter Robertson, who in their own way supported and encouraged my scholarship.

Special thanks also go to the Associate Director and the Director of the Center for Multiethnic and Transnational Studies at the University of Southern California, Professor H. Eric Schockman and Professor Michael B. Preston. I am indebted to these two scholars for my affiliation with the Center. Their support was unconditional. The challenging intellectual and working environment and the interaction with the scholars at the Center added significant contributions to my work. In particular, I am thankful to my colleague Renford Reese, with whom I shared the everyday challenges of scholarship and research. My special thanks also go to Anne Stockemer for her editorial assistance.

Finally, writing a book would not be possible without recognitions, fellowships, scholarships, and awards from institutions interested in a scholar's field of endeavor. For their interest, my thanks go to the following institutions: Institute for the Study of World Politics in Washington, D.C.; The Jewish Vocational Service of Cleveland (Morris Abrams Award in International Relations); and the School of Public Administration, University of Southern California.

1 Ethnic conflict reemerged

The revival of ethnic cleavages and increased tensions is one of the major problems for today's community of nations. Processes of democratization in the aftermath of the Cold War in some countries have revealed old ethnic, religious, and cultural differences and animosities; these have led to the ethnic violence and intrastate wars that jeopardize the traditional concepts of nation-states and world security. The administrative state and state institutions of former socialist states, once relieved of central authoritarian leadership and one-party domination, did not have the capacity to accommodate diverse claims of constituent ethnic groups.

Fundamental assumptions of western democracies about the feasibility of the administrative state to accommodate diversity, which are based on the stability of the greater society on whose behalf it serves and some form of consensus on how that state and its administrative system should operate, may not be valid in the case of former socialist countries. Yugoslavia presents such a case where these fundamentals were lacking, although superficially all looked fine on the surface. All the apologists for Yugoslavia, like Carol Pateman and Ichak Adizes, misled the academic community by merely repeating or justifying the ideological rhetoric on the feasibility of a socialist self-management system to develop the capacity of an administrative state and a broader social and political environment to deal with a diverse multiethnic society.

Horowitz (1985) has used a concept of ethnicity to refer to a highly inclusive (and relatively large scale) group identity based on some notion of common origin, recruited primarily through kinship and typically manifesting some measure of cultural distinctiveness. Ethnicity can embrace groups differentiated by color, language, and religion. It covers tribes, races, nationalities, and castes.

Ethnic conflict is a phenomenon present in all multiethnic societies. It may be manifested in violent or nonviolent forms. Under certain conditions, ethnic conflict may turn to ethnic violence, which can threaten the political and social

1

order of respective nation-states. The worst case scenario happened in the former Yugoslavia (referred to as Yugoslavia). As a result, Yugoslavia disintegrated. The potential for violence, however, exists all over the world. I believe that the violence that has occurred in places such as Yugoslavia presents a serious threat worldwide to peace and security. We all (scholars, practitioners, and citizens) should be concerned and responsible for creating an environment where this kind of conflict can be constrained, contained, and eliminated. For this reason I also believe that the ultimate goal of scholars of ethnic conflict should be to find an answer to prevent the further escalation of ethnic violence in the world. In order to provide support to all parties involved in creating peaceful solutions, it is necessary to create specific models in approaching these kinds of conflicts. To achieve this, one needs to understand the sources of possible ethnic conflicts and both the domestic and the international parties involved.

Ethnic conflict in the world

There are very good reasons why ethnic violence and the challenges of peacemaking should be major preoccupations of scholars and policymakers. Since 170 A.D., there have been 471 wars in each of which at least 1,000 people were killed. Ninety percent of the approximately 100 million deaths recorded in these wars occurred after 1900 (Montville, 1989). A new wave of warfare has occurred in the 1990s, and most of this contemporary violence has a strong ethnic base.

Gellner (1983) reports that there are in the world 8,000 identifiably separate cultures. In addition, according to Albrecht and Forsberg (1995), there are 5,000 groupings that potentially could call for their right of self-determination and their own state. Most of these distinctive groupings are living in multiethnic societies, sharing their state with other groupings. Despite the increased number of independent states created in recent years, multiethnicity remains a dominant feature of most nation-states. Out of 132 independent states in 1971, only 12 (9.1%) were homogeneous from an ethnic point of view (Connor, 1972). With 170 sovereign states in 1989, this situation has not changed. Only Iceland, Norway, and a few others were the exceptions among those 170 sovereign states (Uri Ra'anan, 1989). Presently, with an additional 20 recently emerged nation-states, the situation remains the same.

Ethnic cleavages, which are inherent in the multiethnic character of current dominant nation-state formation, may lead to violent conflict, disintegration, and internationalization of problems at any point in time in almost all societies. With the current progressive trend toward ethnic mobilization and claims for implementation of rights for self-determination, the threat of ethnic violence and war is greater than ever. It should be noted that the achievement of self-determination by one group seldom inspires tolerance on its part for the claims of ethnic minorities that remain within the newly established or claimed boundaries. As argued by Esman (1994), yesterday's victims easily become tomorrow's oppressors. Events in Yugoslavia in the last few years have revealed such a case, where the complexity of a multiethnic society, burdened with historical conflicts and animosities, has led to violence and disintegration of a 70-year-old nation-state. It is necessary to mention that internationalization of ethnic conflict is particularly clear in Yugoslavia's case. The type of ethnic violence that has occurred there is difficult to contain and could easily spill over since it involves stakes in neighboring countries and regions, as well as in regional political and religious organizations.

Some authors see in the decline of nation-states the revival of tribalism and ethno-nationalism. These, in turn, can lead to both violent and nonviolent intrastate conflict, as seen in recent events not only in Yugoslavia but also in Georgia, Azerbaijan, Armenia, Ukraine, Rwanda, Somalia, South Africa, India (Punjab), Sri Lanka, Canada, Belgium, and many other states and regions. Riggs (1994) sees the eruption of ethnonationalist movements in multiethnic states as a modern and growing phenomenon. He identifies three historic tsunamis[1] of nationalism. The first tsunami (the unification and rise of nation-states) culminated in the nineteenth century. It was followed toward the end of the nineteenth century by a second wave, the liberation movements that have continued throughout the twentieth century. The second wave has launched the third (self-determination and ethnonationalism) at the end of the twentieth century. Riggs believes that the third tsunami will probably continue for many decades, if not throughout the twenty-first century, provoking untold human suffering and an unforeseeable end.

Moynihan (1993) recently wrote *Pandaemonium* as a warning to the world, saying, 'It appeared to me that the world was entering a period of ethnic conflict, following the relative stability of the cold war. This could be explained. As large formal structures broke up, and ideology lost its hold, people would revert to more primal identities. Conflict would arise based on these identities' (p. xiii).

For Pfaff (1993), the idea of the ethnic nation is a permanent provocation to war. He argues that the forces at work in a contemporary ethnic war are neither ancient, for the most part, nor incomprehensible. He suggests that supposedly primordial hatreds are a twentieth-century phenomenon, such as in the case of Yugoslavia; further, he believes that Yugoslavia's ethnic war is being waged among three communities possessing no distinct physical characteristics or separate anthropological or racial origins. In his words, 'They are the same people. They have distinct histories, which is another matter' (p. 101).

Kaplan (1994), in his recent article, 'The Coming Anarchy,' in the *Atlantic Monthly*, warns:

> To appreciate fully the political and cartographic implications of postmodernism - an epoch of themeless juxtapositions, in which the classificatory grid of nation-states is going to be replaced by a jagged-grass pattern of city-states, shanty-states, nebulous and anarchic regionalism - it is necessary to consider, finally, the whole question of war. (p. 72)

Authors such as Huntington (1993) go beyond the point of considering purely intrastate violent ethnic conflict as the dominant form of conflict in the next century, arguing that the fundamental source of conflict will occur between civilizations. In his view,

> The great divisions among humankind and the dominating source of conflict will be cultural. Nation-states will remain the most powerful actors in world affairs, but the principal conflicts of global politics will occur between nations and groups of different civilizations. The clash of civilizations will dominate global politics. The fault lines between civilizations will be the battle lines of the future. (p. 22)

Huntington further defines civilization as the highest cultural groupings of people differentiated from each other by history, language, culture, tradition, and, most importantly, religion. He identifies eight major civilizations: Western, Confucian, Japanese, Islamic, Hindu, Slavic-Orthodox, Latin American, and African.

According to most of these authors, and considering today's reality as presented on the evening news, the world could be facing a rather grim future in the twenty-first century. There are many differing recommendations as to what should be done to prevent ethnic warfare and/or the clash of civilizations. For Pfaff (1993), the best solution is to provide NATO guarantees against forcible change of those political frontiers in Eastern, East-Central, and Balkan Europe that have not yet been violated but are threatened because of ethnic claims and rivalries. Riggs (1994) recommends the strategy of promoting democratization in countries burdened by deep cleavages between mutually hostile ethnonations that will lead to viable democratic constitutions. For Huntington (1993), one of the major short-term goals is to prevent escalation of local inter-civilization conflicts into major intercivilization wars, allowing time for the different civilizations to learn to coexist. Cleveland (1993), in his book, *Birth of a New World*, promotes the idea of long-term coexistence between nation-states and civilizations. He presents a comprehensive agenda for peaceful change in this 'open moment' of world history and outlines a detailed strategy for what must be done to 'make the world safe for diversity.'

Understanding ethnic conflict in the world

To deal with ethnic violence and create a better world in the future, it is important first to understand the current situation and the different forces that play important roles in shaping the social, political, and economic environment. It is also critical to investigate and analyze changes of the boundaries of multiethnic nation-states and among the community of nation-states in order to assist current policymakers with proposals and solutions that can lead to reconciliation, peaceful transformation, and coexistence of a community of ethnic groups, nations, states, and civilizations. Since each case of ethnic violence is specific and unique, it needs specific internal and international policy measures. Applying general policy measures without recognizing the specifics of each case may only serve to deepen the conflict instead of solving it.

The Carter Center at Emory University presents an interesting approach to conflict resolution that emphasizes development of strategies and action plans based on identified barriers. These barriers are in each case more or less different and require different strategies (State of the World Conflict Report, 1991-1992). In the case of each particular nation-state and ethnonational movement within it, it is necessary to identify the roots of the conflict: is it historic, ideological, religious, cultural, or imagined? The roots of the conflict matter because it may be that different strategies, policy measures, and actions are required to deal with different root causes.

Most scholars of ethnic conflict have been trying to explain ethnic violence and ethnic cooperation in relation to specific variables. Some of them even like to focus on a particular event, person, or group of people. Such a reductionist approach could be beneficial for scholarship itself, but not for policymakers who have to create domestic and international policies and strategies that are intended to eliminate the contextual factors presenting a fertile field for ethnic violence. In this book I want to explain ethnic violence and ethnic cooperation in relation to a particular composition of variables. I believe that in many cases ethnic violence has occurred due to a specific combination of factors rather than to any one factor. By this I mean that it is impossible to explain ethnic violence and to find a solution for it by looking at only one particular factor. Ethnic mobilization is usually ignited by domestic ethnonational leadership and inappropriate government policy. However, most of the ethnic mobilization movements would not lead to violence if the international community and, in particular, regional political groupings and powers, were not supportive of extreme ethnic group policies and strategies such as unilateral separation by

5

arms and war. Also, ethnic mobilization is less likely to turn to violence if a strong perception of national unity and belief in citizenship and civil and secular society exist.

It seems that the first step in dealing with the problems mentioned above is development of a model that can allow scholars and policymakers to analyze each case with the same concepts, perspectives, and principles. Creating such a model is not an easy task, given the diversity of situations and the uniqueness of each. In chapter three I develop such a model for the study of ethnic conflicts all over the world. Based on this model, the ethnic conflict in Yugoslavia is analyzed. This should increase an understanding of the ethnic violence occurring there and the context in which it has occurred.

Ethnic conflict in Yugoslavia

Events in Yugoslavia and in the world in general in the last few years have revealed the complexity of societies burdened with historic conflicts and animosities. These events have revealed that there is no easy solution for national sociopolitical and economic development and transformation of multiethnic states and societies. In order to highlight Yugoslav specifics that could be in a causal relationship with ethnic violence and disintegration, I trace and analyze the historical development of one nation-state: Yugoslavia. The development of the Yugoslav nation-state has undergone periods of peace and stability as well as periods of violence and wars. Yugoslavia, created in 1918, withstood the challenging period between the two world wars and survived as a monarchy. It survived the Second World War and the rule of Tito. However, it could not survive recent events when ethnonationalism erupted in a period of transition into a multiparty democracy and subsequently turned into violence, war, and disintegration.

The questions addressed in this book include: Why have different ethnic groups, such as Moslems, Croats, and Serbs in Yugoslavia fought each other? Why has violence and war occurred at particular times? What was the domestic and international context in which violence and war erupted? Why in some periods or contexts was the social control of violence successful? And why in some periods or contexts did social controls over violence fail to prevent and stop the destruction? What have been the roles of the domestic polity and the international community in provoking and coping with violent conflicts? And how can national and international organizations and authorities prevent and stop violence?

More specifically, I ask, What are the specific factors that caused war to break out in Croatia, and Bosnia and Herzegovina? Are there specific characteristics of Yugoslav society and the international community that can be underlined as

6

leading to dissolution and war in Yugoslavia, whereas other countries in transition from socialism have avoided this disaster?

Several findings appear to contradict the conventional wisdom regarding the Yugoslav situation. First is that the socialist self-management system 'invented' by Edvard Kardelj[2] and introduced into the Yugoslav political system in 1950 made a significant and largely unrecognized contribution to the ethnic violence and disintegration of Yugoslavia. In this process Yugoslavia was transformed from a community of nations to a community of nation-states through permanent constitutional engineering and decentralization. The political power was gradually shifted over 40 years from the national center to the ethnonational periphery, creating the conditions for development by the republics of extreme ethnocentric policies. This outcome led to ethnic violence and disintegration in a period when an already weakened Yugoslavia tried to transform its socialist self-management system into a multiparty democracy.

Second, the decentralization of Yugoslavia caused by self-management was not a sufficient condition by itself for disintegration. International recognition is one of the major elements in the process of creation of new states and dismemberment of existing states. For example, it is particularly interesting to look at the new international environment following the Cold War era. This new environment has been termed 'The New World Order,' revealing universal values such as self-determination, democracy, human rights guarantees, market economies, nonviolence, and the like. With the new international political environment, however, some regions of longstanding historical conflicts, like Yugoslavia, have been reconfigured and subsequently have turned to violence. It appears that ethnic violence and disintegration of nation-states like Yugoslavia are more likely to occur when the international community is ambiguous concerning the principles on which the world order and recognition of new states are established.

These are not the only causes and conditions affecting Yugoslavia. National complexity, with its many cleavages, has always been a source of potential conflict and violence. Yet, since its inception in 1918, Yugoslavia was a nation comprising many different ethnic, cultural, and religious groups with a long history of peaceful coexistence. Yugoslavia as a state as well as a nation employed different methods and political means to deal with ethnic cleavages. The methods have included formal institutional and regulatory processes (constitution and laws), as well as informal and political methods, including suppression and coercion. Nevertheless, the ethnic groups have never lost their identities. They have always pursued their specific agendas and policies, which in some periods have been compatible with national institutions and policies, while in other periods have been incompatible and conflicting.

To develop these conclusions I used the model in chapter three to identify and analyze conditions which are most likely to be found in a causal relationship with ethnic violence and subsequent national disintegration. In this model, ethnic conflict may be regarded as a dependent variable of domestic, international, perceptual, and systemic independent variables.

I use this model to comparatively assess sources of national cohesion and disintegration since the creation of Yugoslavia in 1918. My analysis specifically deals with the following periods:

- Creation of Yugoslavia in 1918
- Yugoslavia as a monarchy (between the two world wars)
- Second World War and creation of a new Yugoslavia
- Tito's era (from 1945 to 1980)
- Post-Tito era and efforts to transform Yugoslavia (from 1980 to 1990)
- Ethnonationalism, violence, and disintegration in the 1990s

In order to compare outcomes of ethnic conflict in these periods, I examine factors that first led to the integration of different ethnic groups in Yugoslavia in 1918; and that then challenged the existence of the Yugoslav nation and led to its disintegration in 1991.

Based on the research, it is also possible to explore and identify what models of state formation and regulation could fit best for managing ethnic conflict and peaceful transition of complex and mixed societies such as Yugoslavia. It is also possible to explore and identify what role the international community might play in order to provide a smooth transition and mitigate existing conflicts. As such, this research has significance that extends beyond Yugoslavia. It should have significance for security not only in the Balkans and Europe but in the world generally. Ethnic conflicts in societies such as Yugoslavia could have a devastating effect for the whole world and could spread very fast if they are not dealt with in time. The political and administrative capacity of current institutions of the newly created states and regions of Yugoslavia, as well as of international organizations, will play a most important role in solving such conflicts and returning permanent peace to that region.

Organization of the book

This book is divided into eight chapters:

In chapter two I identify and group scholarship on ethnic conflict based on the major theories scholars have used in studying ethnic conflict. These are (1) modernization theory and ethnic conflict, (2) democratic theory and ethnic conflict, (3) nation-building theory and ethnic conflict, (4) theories of nationalism and ethnic conflict, (5) theory of international order and ethnic conflict, and (6) ethnic conflict management.

8

In chapter three I develop a model for comparative study of ethnic conflict that includes domestic, perceptual, systemic, and international variables. In the model these variables are operationalized and concepts are defined.

In chapter four I analyze the perceptual and historic origins of Yugoslavia as well as perceptual and historic origins of Serbian, Croatian, and Moslem ethnonational identities.

In chapter five I analyze the state formation and government regulation of ethnic conflict of Yugoslavia between the two world wars. Ethnic group politics and international conditions are analyzed in particular as the factors that influenced state formation and government regulation of ethnic conflict, followed by the dismemberment of Yugoslavia at the beginning of the Second World War.

In chapter six I analyze ethnic conflict management and ethnic policies in the Second Yugoslavia during the Tito era. International conditions are again assessed from the perspective of state formation and government ethnic policies. This is the period when the socialist self-management experiment in Yugoslavia took place, changing the nature of Yugoslav society and the state.

In chapter seven I examine the period after Tito's death in 1980 that ended with ethnic violence and disintegration in the 1990s. It is a period when the feasibility of the socialist self-management system to adapt itself to the multiparty democracy while providing unity for Yugoslavia was tested. At the end, however, ethnocentric forces and ethnocentric political institutions that developed under the umbrella of self-management prevailed. The tensions among different ethnonational groups in Yugoslavia increased to the point of ethnic violence. Unable to find a negotiated solution within the existing political institutions, leaders of Yugoslav ethnonational groups seeking secession searched for help from the international community. Changes in the international order and the inconsistency of the international community regarding the principles of sovereignty, integrity, and self-determination contributed to the escalation of ethnic violence and to the final disintegration of Yugoslavia.

In chapter eight I provide a summary and conclusions.

Notes

1. Tsunami is the Japanese term for a tidal wave, a metaphor Riggs uses for the processes that have generated vast and violent consequences for the whole world.

2. His concepts resembled the concepts of Guild Socialism already discredited in Great Britain at the beginning of the 1920s.

2 Ethnic conflict in scholarship

Ethnic conflict is the subject of many disciplines. It is studied by political scientists, anthropologists, sociologists, and scholars of organizational behavior, psychology, international relations, economics, government, and administration. The nature of ethnic conflict is such that only an interdisciplinary approach toward its study may be able to produce comprehensive and reliable results.

Many variables and concepts can be examined to explain ethnic conflict. Scholars have tried to identify these variables and concepts and to explain the relationships among them. However, despite their efforts, general theories of ethnic conflict have not been developed, although contextual factors and the diversity of social environments have proved to be important for understanding and explaining ethnic conflict.

Also, most of the scholars of ethnic conflict have studied ethnic conflict exclusively from the national point of view. It is argued by Enloe (1973) that contemporary political scientists may have confined their studies of development to the national unit to such an extent that they mistakenly equate political development with nation-building and thereby overlook political development occurring on other levels. Enloe further argues that two trends are going on simultaneously, each modifying the utility of using the nation as the chief reference point for all political investigators. The first trend is a supranational movement, the emergence of which has perhaps been responsible for neglect of the second trend: the political mobilization of subnational communities. Subnational movements have been relegated to the status of problems for national elites, and frequently have been considered so pathological that they have been handed over to psychologists and sociologists for investigation, while political scientists devote themselves to wielders of power at the center. However, Enloe believes that subnational ethnic mobilization justifies direct study by students of government.

Modernization theory and ethnic conflict

In the literature of the 1950s and 1960s on modernization and ethnic conflict, many scholars argued that economic development, urbanization, and growing literacy would lead to the greater integration of different ethnic groups throughout the world. Modernization theory predicted that greater economic and political interaction among people and modern communication networks would break down ethnic parochial behavior and replace ethnic loyalties with loyalties to larger national, supranational, and global communities. The assumption that ethnic identity will wither away as the processes collectively known as modernization occur came mostly from the writings of Deutch (1966), who claimed that modernization by socially mobilizing large segments of the population would increase both the likelihood and the tempo of their assimilation. Deutch even argued that assimilating diverse ethnic groups is subject to social engineering, noting that, 'Too often men have viewed language and nationality superficially as an accident, or accepted them submissively as fate. In fact they are neither accident nor fate, but the outcome of a discernible process; and as soon as we begin to make the process visible, we are beginning to change it' (p. 164).

Other scholars argued, however, that the relationship between modernization and ethnic groups has been more ambiguous. noting that advances in communication networks have tended to increase the cultural awareness of minority ethnic groups. The impact has been twofold: It has made them more aware of those who share their identities and has also highlighted those who are alien to their ethnic groups (Connor, 1994). Enloe (1973) argues that ethnic identity can be a building block as well as a potential stumbling block on the road to modernity. Political developments in the 1970s, 1980s, and in particular the 1990s have proved to favor Enloe's arguments. Instead of greater integration and more tolerance between ethnic groups, conflicts based on the assertion of ethnic identities have increased sharply (Gurr & Harff, 1994).

Increased ethnic awareness and ethnic mobilization (in some cases ethnic militancy) may take two directions: toward greater national cohesiveness, based on more equal distribution of power, or toward a devolution of power in order to meet the aspirations of ethnic groups that cannot be absorbed by national institutions. The latter is more likely to happen if the ethnic groups have been more resistant to assimilation tendencies of modernization and to the formation of broader identities. Devolution of power could take several forms. It could lead to decentralization, or it could produce autonomy for smaller political units (Enloe, 1973). It could also lead to disintegration and civil war.

Scholars have used several alternative approaches to explain the persistence of ethnic conflict in the contemporary world. Advocates of the primordial perspective on ethnic conflict hold that people's ethnic identities have deep social, historical, and genetic foundations. From this perspective, modernization is considered as a threat to ethnic solidarity and culture. On the other hand, advocates of the instrumental nature of ethnic mobilization maintain that the main goals of a group are assumed to be material and political gains and that the ethnic identity is used only as a means to attain those goals. Gurr and Harff (1994) argue that, using this perspective, the most important effect of modernization is to increase economic differences, or awareness of and resentment toward differences, between dominant groups and minorities. Political leadership tends to capitalize on these differences by creating ethnically based political movements. One such argument, called internal colonialism, was used to explain growing ethnic conflict in some countries, particularly in developed European societies - for example, the regional separatist movements like those of the Welsh and Scots in Britain, the Bretons and Corsicans in France, and the Basques in Spain.

In explaining ethnic conflict, advocates of the primordial and instrumental perspectives have been using different factors. The advocates of the primordial perspective have emphasized the importance of ethnic identity, culture, and bounds, while advocates of instrumental perspective have emphasized the pursuit of material and political interests. The two theories are not, however, fundamentally inconsistent. Gurr and Harff (1994) think that ethnic groups are most likely to mobilize when both conditions - a strong sense of ethnic group identity in combination with imposed disadvantages - are present. A common argument is that when peoples of different ethnic groups compete directly for the same scarce resources and positions, their ethnic identities become more important to them. And if some groups are more successful than others, inequalities increase, thus providing the second general condition for ethnic mobilization and conflict. More and more, scholars tend to incorporate both conditions.

Democratic theory and ethnic conflict

The major question for which scholars have been trying to find an answer is whether ethnic pluralism and democracy can be reconciled. Democracy is a form of government with institutionalized competition and conflict. Democracy requires ethnic conflict to be managed peacefully and constitutionally within the boundaries of equality, decency, an agreed institutional order, and restraint. Scholars and politicians have been divided about the possibility of democracy succeeding in severely divided societies. In 1861 John Stuart Mill reasoned that democracy is next to impossible in a country made up of different nationalities. Diamond and Platter (1994) are convinced that ethnicity is the most difficult type of cleavage for a democracy to manage, because ethnicity taps cultural and

12

symbolic issues - basic notions of identity and the self, of individual and group worth and entitlement, such as glorification of a national language - that cannot be broken down into bargainable increments. The conflicts generated are intrinsically less amenable to compromise than those revolving around material issues. It is particularly clear when competing notions of morality - of the sacred and the profane - are invoked, as in the conflicts that involve religion.

Some scholars agree that, in deeply divided societies, ethnicity is the factor that determines who will be granted and who will be denied access to power and resources. Democratic elections take on the character of a 'census,' where one ethnic group or coalition of ethnic groups (parties) wins by its sheer demographic weight while others lose, often being excluded from the government and the larger political community. That is why many scholars have expressed concern and skepticism about the possibility of a stable democracy in societies where ethnicity has become politicized (Diamond & Platter, 1994; Horowitz, 1985). Nevertheless, optimism prevails in the writings of some scholars. For example, Horowitz, despite the concerns, has concluded that no case is to be made for the futility of democracy or the inevitability of uncontrolled ethnic conflict. Even in the most severely divided societies, ties of blood do not lead ineluctably to ethnic violence. Also, Riggs, mentioned earlier, recommends the strategy of promoting democratization in countries burdened by deep cleavages between hostile ethno-nations. Dahl (1971) emphasizes the importance of accommodative elite practices that ensure some minimal level of protection so that a defeat in elections will not mean total or permanent exclusion from power and resources.

There are many ways to manage ethnic conflict in ethnically divided countries. Most scholars, though, agree that timing is critical (Horowitz, 1994). Once deep ethnic divisions are mobilized into electoral and party politics, it may be too late to build trust and tolerance, civility and accommodation. In such societies suspicion, acrimony, and polarization prevail. Often these lead to ethnic violence, civil war, and disintegration.

In commenting on procedures needed to build a stable democracy in an ethnically divided society, Diamond and Platter (1994) advise that it is critical to create political institutions and party systems that offer incentives for accommodation rather than polarization. Particularly in emerging democracies, deliberate constitutional engineering is a vital tool of ethnic conflict management. One of the means by which democracies manage and contain conflict is through the generation of cross-cutting cleavages. Interaction of the people along a different line of cleavage, such as class, tends to moderate their ethnic behavior and induces greater tolerance and accommodation. The authors suggest that it is easier to cross ethnic boundaries when they are not maintained by clear physical markings. In some ethnically plural societies, ethnicity may be just one among several identities an individual may possess. Also, ethnic boundaries may disappear over time through intermarriage. Unfortunately, in some divided societies, ethnic cleavages have proved particularly rigid and enduring despite modernization, democratization, intermarriage, and the like. Societies of the former Soviet Union and Eastern Europe are within the groups affected the most by the rigidity of ethnic cleavages.

Nation building theory and ethnic conflict

Scholars associated with theories of nation-building have mostly ignored the question of ethnic conflict or considered it superficially as a minor impediment to effective nation-state integration. Scholars of nation-building consider ethnic identity as somewhat unimportant; they feel that it will be replaced by the common identity of a nation-state as communication networks advance and link the state's various ethnic groups more closely. Connor (1994) holds that undue optimism has dominated the scholarship on nation-building.

Scholars of nation-building see the fundamental role of the state in multiethnic societies as elaborating and resolving the contradiction of differentiation and unity. The use of force and disciplinary power of the state are regarded as the means for protecting cultural diversity within the nation while at the same time perpetuating national unity.

The premise is also held that nation-building processes should be interwoven into the concept of the nation-state, embedded in its institutions, policies and practices, and organized and executed through state bureaucracies. Nationalism is regarded as a part of nation-building processes. As a politicized language or ideology of national unity, it has been heavily used by party, state, and administrative leadership and politicians in projects of identity construction that focus on the nation. It is considered to be an ideology of identity that advocates the belief that national identity is fundamental and natural (Bash, Schiller, & Blanc, 1994). Since the French Revolution, concepts and practices of traditional institutions have repeatedly been challenged by nationalist (nation-building) leadership and movements in different parts of the world. Mayall (1990) believes that at one level of analysis this challenge has been enormously successful. The ultimate measure of that success is the difficulty that people everywhere have in envisaging an alternative political form to that of the nation-state. Yet, today this political form is challenged more than ever by supra- and subnational forces. Nation-states have been resistant to change so far. Nonetheless, some of them, such as Yugoslavia, have already disintegrated with efforts to form smaller nation-states. Others, such as the European Union, are on the road to integration in larger regional organizations.

Theories of nationalism and ethnic conflict

In this chapter I deal with the theoretical formulation of nationalism. Since details are critical for studying ethnic conflict, in later chapters I deal more specifically with some concepts of nationalism. Different concepts have been used to explain nationalism in Central and Eastern Europe and nationalism in Western Europe. The origins of nationalism are associated with western enlightenment and the idea of people's sovereignty. When used in the contexts of Central and Eastern Europe, however, the concept of nationalism is considered chiefly as an indicator of hegemonic ideologies and movements.

As explained by Griffiths (1993), the difference lies in the relationship between homogeneity of populations and the development of the nation-state. Griffiths notes that in Western Europe the creation of nation-states was made easier by the relative achievement of national homogeneity in the eighteenth and nineteenth centuries. This happened because large-scale migrations had ceased in Western Europe by the start of the nineteenth century and because the Roman Catholic Church had acted as a funnel of assimilation since the early Middle Ages. In Central and Eastern Europe, according to Griffiths, nationalism appeared at a more backward stage of social and political development, when the borders of eastern states were still fluid and migrations, sometimes forced, continued into the twentieth century.

Gellner (1983) has highlighted the adaptive and evolutionary qualities of the understanding of nationalism, particularly with regard to Central Europe. In a recent article he describes how nationalism has passed through five stages, each producing different forms of nationalism in the regions of Central and Eastern Europe since 1815: from the European empires following the Congress of Vienna, through the 'nationalist irredentism' of the late nineteenth century, the triumph of nationalism after Versailles in 1918, the 'homogenization' process of Adolf Hitler and Joseph Stalin after 1939 and the totalitarian regimes of 1945 to 1989, and, finally, the present period (in Griffiths, 1993, pp. 12-13).

For the purpose of this study it is important to make a reference to the Marxist-Leninist theory of nationalism and nations, since Marxist-Leninist ideology has been used as the basis for social and national engineering in Central and Eastern Europe since the Second World War. In Marxist literature the most significant social cleavage is the one between socioeconomic classes. Marxism predicted that ethnic cleavages (nationalities) would disappear with the development of socialist forces. It was argued that the nation is a historically evolved phenomenon that came into existence only with the demise of feudalism and the rise of capitalism as a result of changes in the mode of production. Nationalism was considered as mainly a device of the bourgeoisie for identifying their class interests as the interests of the entire society (Connor, 1984).

Connor further details the major propositions of Marx and Engels' position on nationalism as follows:

1. The nation and its ideology (nationalism) are part of the superstructure, byproducts of the capitalist era.

2. Nationalism is therefore an ephemeral phenomenon which will not survive capitalism.

3. Nationalism can be progressive or reactionary force, the watershed for any society being a point of developed capitalism.

4. Whether progressive or reactionary, nationalism is everywhere a bourgeois ideology pressed into service by that class in order to divert the proletariat from realizing its own class consciousness and interests.

5. This stratagem cannot work, for loyalties are determined by economic realities rather than by ethnonational sentiments.

6. Communists may support any movement, nationalist or otherwise, when the movement represents the most progressive alternative.

7. But Communists themselves must remain above nationalism, this immunity being their single defining characteristic. (pp. 10-11)

Lenin conceived of nationalism in purely negative terms and used the rhetoric of self-determination to combat nationalism. He argued that the right to self-determination is an exception from the general promise of centralism. However, the right to self-determination was not expected to be used within a communist state. Again, Connor describes the basic elements of Lenin's strategy to combat nationalism as follows:

1. Prior to the assumption of power, promise to all national groups the right of self-determination (expressly including the right of secession), while proffering national equality to those who wish to remain within the state.

2. Following the assumption of power, terminate the fact - though not process of assimilation via the dialectical route of territorial autonomy for all compact nation groups.

3. Keep the party centralized and free of all nationalist proclivities. (p. 38)

This third and final prescription of Lenin to combat nationalism was implemented throughout the Communist Party organization. Lenin expected that the principle of strict centralization (democratic centralism) was the best protection of unity against nationalism.

For a better understanding of nationalism and the role nationalism plays in one society, it is important to identify the different forms that nationalism can take. Forms of nationalism are assessed in relation to ethnic conflict as identified and elaborated by Griffiths (1993). These are:

1. Sub-state nationalism, such as that of the Slovaks or Croatians. This is also known as potential state nationalism.

2. Pan-nationalism, which is used in the context of Pan-Turkism or Greater Turkestan, as movements to unify in a single cultural political community several states on the basis of shared cultural characteristics or a family of cultures.

3. Hyper-state nationalism, which is used to refer to the nationalism of states like Serbia.

4. Positive nationalism, which does not contradict the pursuit of democratization, and is beneficial for binding a population through processes of transformation and modernization - for example, the United States, France, and the United Kingdom.

5. Trans-border ethnic disputes, such as those of the Hungarians in the border lands of Hungary proper.

6. Sub-state ethnic conflict, especially in the republics of the former Yugoslavia, or the former Soviet Union. (p. 14)

Theory of international order and ethnic conflict

The historical framework for this book is relatively short, focusing on significant changes in the international order since 1918. The global political environment in particular has changed in the last decade of the twentieth century. As a result of the willingness of the international community to intervene through the United Nations and other means in what was formerly considered an internal matter of the existing state , ethnic conflicts have became more sensitive to the political and economic restructuring of the international community. Causal relationships can be identified among new alliances, aspirations, and ethnic violence in many areas of the world.

To understand the importance of the international order in regulating ethnic conflict, Mayall (1990) has proposed that one should try to answer these questions: Under what circumstances is the nationalist challenge and its claims for restructuring the old order and states most likely to succeed? Is that territorial revision very rare? What are the circumstances conducive to it? The three great waves of modern state creation have been associated with the collapse of empires (in Latin America in the nineteenth century, in Europe after 1919, and in the developing world after 1945). Mayall notes that no more empires remain to collapse and, therefore, that very limited possibilities for further state creation exist by this route. Recent changes in the former Soviet Union, Yugoslavia, and some other countries appear not to support Mayall's arguments.

At the Versailles Peace Conference in 1918, President Woodrow Wilson of the United States failed to dictate the ultimate terms of peace and the new world order. He had, however, an enormous influence on the general shape of the world which emerged. Wilson made the principle of national self-determination the basis of his plan for a new international order. He considered that there was no gap between national self-determination and democracy. He also advocated the idea of a self-policing system of collective security to replace the system of international power politics. The central problem with his vision on which the League of Nations was based, according to Mayall (1990), lay in its failure to confront the problem of power as an enduring reality rather than as an anachronistic feature of the old order. The implementation of his plan also confronted an immediate problem of a more practical nature, namely, the problem of minorities. This problem was particularly obvious in the case of the Balkan states, where the principle of self-determination was compromised and never fully implemented.

The 1918 design for a new world order was significant, nevertheless, as Mayal (1990) points out. After 1918 the dominant political form became the nation-state rather than the multinational empire. In addition, the process of national self-determination began almost as soon as national self-determination was advanced after 1918 as the new principle of international legitimacy. It involved, first, equating the popular principle of sovereignty with the attack on the remaining dynastic empires in Europe, and later after the Second World War with anticolonialism generally. Second, it favored political settlements in settling disputed claims.

Since the 'Great War' took a devastating toll on the nations of Europe, the international community sought to establish a new global organization that would prevent such a war from taking place in the future. The League of Nations was established in 1919 as the result of these efforts. After the First World War, however, the polarization among the membership about the role of the League of Nations and concepts of war prevention made this organization inefficient and incapable of dealing with threats when they arose.

When powerful threats to the peace appeared, such as the Japanese incursion into Manchuria, the Italian attack on Ethiopia, and the German annexations of the Rhineland, Austria, and Czechoslovakia, the League of Nations proved incapable of stopping these aggressions. The punitive elements of the Treaty in Versailles and the impotence of the League led inevitably to the Second World War, which brought unprecedented suffering to humankind. As Luard (1982) describes it, the League had been designed to implement the principle of 'collective security.' The League Covenant declared, in Article 11, that 'any war or threat of war, whether immediately affecting any of the members of the League or not, is hereby declared a matter of concern to the whole League'; and in Article 10 it laid down the principle that 'therefore the members of the League undertake to respect and preserve as against external aggression the territorial integrity and existing political independence of all members of the League' (pp. 4-5). Despite these measures, the principle of collective security was never put into effect.

Luard further claims that the League collapsed because it had no 'teeth.' For him the idea that the League should possess forces of its own had been too revolutionary to be seriously entertained at the time of its foundation, and that in general the prerogatives of national sovereignty were still far too deeply cherished at the time the League was founded. He emphasizes that it was almost everywhere taken for granted that national governments must retain control of their own forces and must themselves determine whether or not they should be committed to any particular collective action to defeat aggression.

Some lessons drawn from the experience and failure of the League of Nations, according to Luard, were: (1) A more universal body was needed. The United States had never belonged to the League of Nations. Germany belonged only for a brief period between 1926 and 1933. The Soviet Union belonged for a still shorter time, between 1934 and her expulsion in 1939. Italy and Japan left in the early thirties. A huge area of the world, then still under colonial rule, possessed no voice at all in the organization. (2) The rule of unanimity that had prevailed in the League must be abandoned.

From the beginning of the Second World War it was clear that a new international organization would be needed at its end. Plans for a new organization to replace the ineffective League of Nations began to be made from 1942 onwards. On 1 January 1942, 26 states, which had established an alliance against the Axis after the United States and other countries entered the war, reaffirmed this declaration and named themselves the United Nations. Statements in speeches increasingly referred in general terms to the new world order to be created at the war's conclusion (Luard, 1982).

The major event during the Second World War concerning the future world order took place at Yalta in February 1945. Unfortunately, the Crimea Conference of the Big Three held at Yalta was not successful in establishing a shared vision of the postwar order (Holsti, 1991). The prime consideration of Churchill, Roosevelt, and Stalin was to maintain unity for the prosecution of the war and to develop some common understandings about the postwar order. The differences in perception of the postwar order were so significant, however, that already at that time it was clear that little prospect remained for extending wartime collaboration into peacetime. The theories of peace of the Big Three were largely incompatible. This incompatibility led to a long period of the Cold War, which dominated international relations from the Second World War to 1989.

Despite the differences between the major powers that led to the Cold War, reason prevailed among them in conceptualizing an international peace and security system. At the United Nations Conference of International Organizations in San Francisco, on 26 June, 1945, 51 states signed the United Nations Charter and delegated to the United Nations the power to maintain international peace and security. The new system appeared in many ways an advance over that established in the League of Nations. It included all major powers in its membership, and the universal veto available within the League on Nations, which had weakened its effectiveness, was replaced by limited veto power, restricted to the permanent members alone (Luard, 1982).

The United Nations system established in 1945 outlived the Cold War. It was more or less capable of dealing with interstate conflicts, but in the aftermath of the Cold War the United Nations system was unable to adjust fast enough to combat the phenomenon of ethnic violence within states revealed by the new world order. The assumed sanctity of existing nation-state boundaries meant that major ethnic demands for new boundaries (e.g., Basques, Kurds, etc.) could not be dealt with. These were internal, not international, issues. Scholars of peace and security agree that the new concepts of peace and security, as well as of institutions and policies, are needed to make the United Nations capable of bringing and maintaining peace in war-torn regions.

Ethnic conflict management

Scholars of ethnic conflict management have been trying to explain the occurrence of ethnic violence in relation to particular ethnic group strategies and government policies. The objective is to identify the strategies that could prevent ethnic violence and /or reconcile the differences among ethnic groups, particularly majority versus minority ethnic groups. Gurr and Harff (1994) point out that the mobilization of ethnic groups is the immediate precursor of political actions used to make demands on governments. The extent, intensity, and form of conflict among the ethnic groups and these groups and governments depend upon the policies and strategies advocated and implemented by leaders of ethnic groups and of those created and followed by governments.

The diversity and complexity of ethnic conflicts place limitations on the development of a general theory of ethnic conflict management. Horowitz has argued that any single formula for conflict management is not universal enough to incorporate all cases and forms of ethnic conflict (in Diamond & Platter, 1994). Lijphart (1977) has proposed a consociational formula to manage the ethnic cleavages of deeply divided societies. His formula involves power-sharing arrangements with four key features: grand coalitions, mutual veto, proportionality, and segmental autonomy and federalism. To the contrary, Horowitz is of the view that the consociational model is seriously flawed. He is suspicious about grand, all-inclusive governing coalitions, saying that a grand coalition is inherently unsustainable amidst the political tensions and jealousies of deep ethnic divisions. Also, he sees consociational formulas as least useful in cases where elite traditions and motivations for accommodation are not developed, as in the case with European countries like the Netherlands, on which Lijphart's consociational model has been developed.

Most scholars of ethnic conflict acknowledge the importance of federalism, or some substantial devolution of power, as an instrument for democratic ethnic conflict management. Horowitz (In D & P, 1994) believes that the key issue is to design political institutions so as to make moderation pay. The ideal arrangement, according to him, may be a system of competing multiethnic coalitions that alternate in power over time. Federalism has an enormous potential value as a tool for managing, containing, and reducing ethnic conflict. Federalism is pivotal because it can perform important functions to reduce ethnic conflict. It has the potential to disperse conflict, create incentives and opportunities for interethnic cooperation, encourage alignments on nonethnic interests, and , through redistribution from the center to state and even local governments, reduce material disparities among ethnic groups. However, it is important to be clear about how federalism is structured and implemented. The first question to be answered is whether to create homogeneous or heterogeneous subfederal units. A second key issue is the number of subfederal units.

Ethnic conflict management, according to its character, can take both extreme and moderate forms. Also, in order to emphasize the different objectives of ethnic conflict management, some scholars divide policies into two groups, one to eliminate differences and another to manage it (McGarry & O'Leary, 1993).

Horowitz (1990) was trying to analyze what policies have been or might be used to foster accommodation. He believes that quite a number exist at the extremes, such as secession or partition. Both of these policies involve homogenization. Horowitz also suggests that partition and secession have additional problems, often converting what was domestic ethnic conflict into a more dangerous international ethnic conflict. In addition, new forms of ethnic conflict emerge from partition or secession. Separating out one group does not separate out all the groups, and the problem of ethnic conflict remains. He proposes that, if two ethnic groups cannot live together, perhaps it is better for them to separate. However, separation should be a policy of last resort.

Another way to accommodate ethnic conflict, according to Horowitz, is homogenization by means of assimilation or loss of ethnic group identity. The most extreme accommodation method is homogenization by extermination. He also believes that assimilation is not a good short-term policy; rather it is a long-term business that takes decades or centuries. That is why, when policymakers adopt assimilation as a short-term policy, they typically produce a separatist reaction among such groups. Assimilationist policies tend to backfire.

More promising methods of ethnic conflict management are based on structural techniques that change the institutional format in which conflict occurs, focusing on alternation of the structure of incentives for political actors. Horowitz suggests that the main structural techniques have to do with the apportionment of territory (federalism and regional autonomy) and electoral systems. Many territorial and electoral innovations may be used to manage ethnic conflict. To avoid the rule where one winner takes command of a whole region, federalism can redistribute the power by making and remaking legislative majorities and minorities through adjusting the territories in which their votes are to be counted.

In introducing electoral innovations, it is necessary to keep in mind that in severely divided societies, political parties tend to break along ethnic lines. Given this fact, Horowitz elaborated five goals that can be pursued profitably through the electoral system in managing ethnic conflict. The first involves the A-B, 60-40 problem. In such a case, the objective is to try to fragment the support of the majority group in order to prevent it from achieving permanent domination. Fragmentation is the most difficult goal to accomplish, having been used without success in Guyana in 1964. Second, one might wish to induce an ethnic group to behave moderately toward another group and engage in interethnic bargaining. To achieve this objective it is most important to build incentives for moderation. Moderation was successfully achieved in some periods in Nigeria and Sri Lanka.

Third, one might wish to encourage the formation of multiethnic political organizations. Unfortunately, not enough has been done to facilitate these sorts of arrangements. Fourth, one might wish to preserve a measure of fluidity or multipolar balance among several groups to prevent bifurcation. Avoiding bifurcation by preserving fluidity is an objective the electoral system might foster. It is difficult to achieve since it depends on ability to fragment the groups by the electoral process. Fifth, it might be advisable to reduce the disparity between votes won and seats won (proportionality). It was achieved temporarily in Guyanese elections in 1964. Distributive policies are additional techniques in which the objective is to alter the ethnic balance of rewards and opportunities. These techniques involve preferential policies of recruitment in the public or private sector, business licenses, contracts, share ownership, and the like (Horowitz, 1990).

In many cases ethnic conflict management cannot be achieved through the existing constitutions. Constitutions serve many purposes. They ordain the uses of power by creating such institutions of government as a parliament, executive, and courts. They channel government's power and put limits on it. Some constitutions, such as the United States Constitution, live a long time. The United States Constitution was drafted in 1787 and, with its amendments, remains in force today. Other constitutions are short-lived. Since 1789 France has had seventeen constitutions. Ethnic violence, civil wars, regime changes, and the like tend to trigger the making of a constitution. The Yugoslav crisis and the collapse of the Soviet Union have brought just such a time of constitution-making to the countries of Central and Eastern Europe.

The dawn of a new era requires constitutions that reflect the premises of a democratic society in which the rule of law replaces the rule of the party. But in many cases, formal constitutional changes are not sufficient to accommodate informal and real power structures. Sometimes introduction of a new constitution means nothing more than listing of unattainable objectives, or copies of constitutions from other countries that do not reflect the real power structure and governing processes. It should be recalled that, before the United States Constitution was adopted in 1787, Americans had lived through more than a century of trial and error in establishing the foundations of an enduring constitutionalism (Howard, 1993).

Conclusions

The explanatory power of the theories reviewed and of ethnic conflict management policies is limited when one wants to explain causes and conditions of ethnic violence and disintegration. Modernization and democratization can lead to both integration and polarization of multiethnic societies. Nation-building and nationalism could be important means for creating of national unity in a multiethnic society, while extreme ethnonationalism can lead to ethnic violence and disintegration. The international order has always been an important factor in regulating ethnic conflict. Whenever principles on which international order is established are ambiguous, it is most likely that ethnic violence and disintegration will occur, but not necessarily if other conditions are not prone to ethnic violence. In an overview of ethnic conflict management policies, one can find that any single formula for ethnic conflict management is not universal enough to incorporate all forms of ethnic conflict. As such, ethnic violence can occur if the perceptual, domestic, and international nature of specific ethnic conflict is not understood and appropriate policies to deal with it are not developed.

All of these theories inform my argument. Their individual explanatory potential, however, is limited since they deal only with some of the conditions that eventually can lead eventually to ethnic violence. The assumption of this study is that for ethnic violence to occur, multiple conditions must be present, such as extreme ethnonationalism along with ambiguous policies in the international community.

3 Model for comparative study of ethnic conflict

The limited potential of the theories elaborated in the second chapter to explain ethnic violence and disintegration suggests the need to develop a model that can be used for a comparative study of ethnic conflict.

Model

Four main levels of analysis are used for the explanations of ethnic conflict (see model on the right). My model emphasizes the following groups of explanatory factors: (1) systemic, (2) domestic, (3) perceptual, and (4) international.

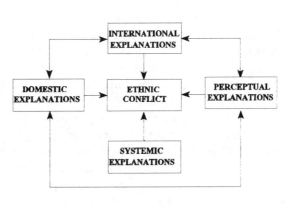

Ethnic conflict may be regarded as a dependent variable with a range of possible outcomes from ethnic violence to ethnic accommodation. Ethnic violence itself may lead to civil war and disintegration or repression and coercive integration. Ethnic accommodation may lead to peaceful disintegration or a peaceful integrative solution.

The independent explanatory variables are as follows:

1. Systemic - ethnic cleavages.

2. Domestic - state formation, state regulation of ethnic conflict, ethnic group mobilization, and ethnic policies.

3. Perceptual - national identity and ethnic group identity.

4. International - the world order and principles regarding self determination and sovereignty of existing states.

Operationalization of variables, theory and definition of concepts

Concepts such as nation, nationalism, nation-state, ethnonationalism, and self-determination are used heavily by politicians and scholars throughout the world in their efforts to formulate policy dealing with problems such as violence, ethnic conflict, civil war, democratization, peaceful transition, and the like. Often these terms have significantly or subtly different meanings and connotations depending on who is using the term and for what purpose. That is why in this chapter an effort is made to define and operationalize these major concepts consistently, after which they can be used in the model for the study of particular cases, such as the case of Yugoslavia.

A beginning can be made by examining the concepts of nation, nation-state, nationalism, ethnic group, ethnocentrism (ethnonationalism), self-determination, ethnic autonomy, and social and ethnic stratification in order to sort out how these terms have been used and what their actual referents are in the world. For example, Pffaf (1993) states that one can separate the history from the defining characteristics of an ethnic group.

There are many theories that define ethnic groups and other phenomena, but no general theories of ethnic groups apply in all cases. Some theories are closer to the realities of particular cases, but not appropriate to others. Identifying the elements within a particular case could help to develop arguments in favor of or against particular theories. Also, it is necessary to emphasize that different major assumptions can lead to different solutions. (For example, Hobbes[1] and Locke[2] provide major examples of two different perspectives based on two different assumptions of a state of nature.) Scholars and policymakers who have assumptions closer to those of Hobbes would advocate more coercive policies, while those who have assumptions closer to Locke's would advocate more civic solutions.

One of the most comprehensive frameworks for conceptualizing the issues of ethnicity and nationalism is found in a recent work by Kellas, *The Politics of Nationalism and Ethnicity* (1991). The central aim of his book is to provide an integrated theory of the politics of nationalism and ethnicity. He developed a synopsis of theory using the sections to represent a 'building block' of the theory, where each 'building block' is built upon foundations of its predecessor. For each 'building block' the relevant academic disciplines are given. In the end he provides a synopsis composed of five 'building blocks': human nature and political behavior; ideas and ideologies; cultural, economic, social, and political change; consociational democracy; and nationalism in international relations.

Despite his efforts, a framework viable for research cannot be developed without first defining the concepts and phenomena being dealt with. Kellas uses a glossary of concepts and terms in the study of ethnicity prepared by Riggs (1985). In this study, Riggs's major definitions of nation, nationalism, ethnic group, ethnocentrism, and ethnicity are used; also, definitions from other major scholars in the field are used to present the concepts and phenomena as interpreted from different perspectives.

In my model, the following concepts need further elaboration and operationalization:

1. Ethnic conflict
   Ethnic violence
   Civil war and disintegration
   Repression and coercive integration
   Ethnic accommodation
   Peaceful disintegration
   Peaceful integration

2. Systemic explanations
   Ethnic cleavages

3. Domestic explanations
   The effectiveness of states in regulating ethnic conflict
   The impact of ethnic group politics and ethnic mobilization on state stability

4. Perceptual explanations
   History and origins of national identity, and nation-building processes
   History and origins of ethnic groups' identities, and ethnocentrism

5. International explanations
   Changes in the world order and the role of the United Nations (the League of Nations) in regulating intrastate ethnic conflicts
   Development of principles of self-determination vs. territorial integrity and sovereignty of existing states

Ethnic conflict

The term conflict itself needs more qualification. Albrecht and Forsberg (1995) indicate that the term conflict is usually used to express armed struggle. In their view, the fact that conflict is a constitutive aspect of all human societies, including democratic, is often ignored. Based on this conceptualization of conflict, ethnic conflict should not be considered exclusively as a violent event. Ethnic conflict may be manifested as either violent or nonviolent phenomena.

   Ethnic violence can occur as a result of many types of internal conflict. Rupesinge (1992) recognizes four types of internal conflicts that generally result in serious or violent hostilities. These are (1) ideological conflicts between states and insurgent movements; (2) governance and authority conflicts concerning the distribution of power and authority in society; (3) racial conflicts; and (4) identity conflicts where the dominant aspect is ethnic, religious, tribal, or linguistic difference or self-determination and devolution of power. These conflicts are often called protracted social conflicts or intractable conflicts. In many cases of ethnic violence, several types of conflicts have actually been waged simultaneously. This is particularly true in the case of societies in transition where democratization and identity crises occur simultaneously.

Ethnic violence (violent ethnic conflict)

Civil war and disintegration In many cases, ethnic groups have not been able to agree on a new constitutional arrangement or peaceful separation. Such ethnic disputes subsequently become violent, some escalating into all-out interethnic wars. These ethnic wars, in fact resemble civil wars occurring along the lines of ethnic cleavages. The final result of such civil wars is disintegration of the existing sovereign multiethnic state and creation of new smaller states. The tendency is to create monoethnic states. However, since such an ideal type' is not achievable in reality, most new states present new political entities in which a former minority becomes the majority in order to dominate other ethnic groups that remain within the boundaries of new states.

Repression and coercive integration In many multiethnic states, particularly in those with authoritarian regimes in power, the state has a tendency to use

28

coercive methods to stop ethnic violence and safeguard the territorial integrity of the existing sovereign state. In extreme cases the state uses martial law, police, and military forces to prevent and/or stop violence. In many cases changes are made toward a more authoritarian and centralized state, leading to a severe violation of human rights. Most socialist countries have used this method in the process of nation-building, as have many developing and some West European countries in periods of ethnic tensions and violence.

Ethnic accommodation (nonviolent ethnic conflict)

Peaceful disintegration Czechoslovakia is a example of this approach. Domestic and international political institutions have been used for harmonization of ethnic conflict. The process of separation is conducted exclusively through negotiation and mediation.

Peaceful integration Ethnic conflict is solved through the process of ethnic conflict management and accommodation within the existing multiethnic state. Claims of different ethnic groups are met through bargaining among ethnic groups and government. Bargaining is the process that leads toward a new constitution, state formation, more political, administrative, and cultural autonomy, and the like. More or less this is the process now going on in former multiethnic socialist countries that have succeeded in avoiding large-scale violence in the process of democratization and transformation. It is also possible to make ethnic cleavages less salient through the use of cross-cutting cleavages in order to moderate ethnic demands.

Systemic explanations

Ethnic cleavages To deal with ethnic cleavages I will use concepts of ethnicity, ethnic nations, ethnic stratification, and cleavages developed and used by Donald L. Horowitz (1985), Milton J. Esman (1994), Tamotsu Shibutani and Kian M. Kwan (1965), and Douglas W. Rae and Michael Taylor (1970).
   Horowitz (1985), as mentioned earlier, has used concepts of ethnicity to refer to a highly inclusive (and relatively large scale) group identity based on some notion of common origin, recruited primarily through kinship and typically manifesting some measure of cultural distinctiveness. Ethnicity can embrace groups differentiated by color, language, and religion. It covers tribes, races, nationalities, and castes. Horowitz speculates that group boundaries may shift as groups divide, merge, and redefine themselves over time (in part by recasting or reinventing myths of common origin).
   The concept of ethnic nation is used by Esman (1994) to emphasize the difference between ethnic community and ethnic nation. He defines ethnic

nation as a politicized ethnic community whose spokesmen demand control over what they define as their territorial homeland, either in the form of substantial autonomy or complete independence. Esman defines ethnic community in a way that is essentially the same as Horowitz. An ethnic community is a group of people united by inherited culture, racial features, belief system (religions), or national sentiments. Membership in an ethnic community is normally an ascriptive phenomenon, a relationship into which the individual is born.

Shibutani and Kwan (1965) emphasize that the theory of ethnic stratification can be derived from broad sociological generalization about social structure. According to them the population in most communities is heterogenous, the people being divided along class, religious, or ethnic lines. For them the relationship between such groups varies; it may be one of coexistence, stratification, or sustained opposition. In their words:

> Those who occupy the same habitat, however, sooner or later become involved in a common web of life; in most cases they participate in a common economic system. Ethnic stratification is one aspect of community organization; individuals are placed in a hierarchical order, not in terms of their personal aptitudes but in terms of their supposed ancestry. An ethnic group consists of people who conceive of themselves as being alike by virtue of common ancestry, real or fictitious, and are so regarded by others. Where a color line develops, the fate of an individual depends upon the manner in which he is classified. The color line is a particular type of social structure, and a theory of ethnic stratification therefore can be derived from broad sociological generalization about social structures. (p. 572)

According to Rae and Taylor (1970), cleavages are the criteria that divide the members of a community into groups, and the relevant cleavages are those dividing members into groups with important political differences at specific times and places. They identify three general classes of cleavages: (1) ascriptive or trait cleavages such as race or caste; (2) attitudinal or opinion cleavages such as ideology or, less grandly, preference; and (3) behavioral or act cleavages such as those elicited through voting and organizational membership. They emphasize that cleavage by traits determines the heterogeneity or homogeneity of a community, while cleavage by attitude determines the extent of dissensus or consensus in community, and cleavage by behavior determines the fractionalization or cohesion of a community. (This is specified based on a type of criteria with low cleavage extreme: homogeneity, consensus, and cohesion, and high cleavage extreme: heterogeneity, dissensus, and fractionalization.)

There are many ways for ethnic groups to differentiate themselves one from another. It can be done in reference to origin and kinship as well as to culture, religion and/or nationality. The most important concern for this study, however, is to identify ways to recognize the difference between ethnic groups and ethnic nations. As argued by Esman, ethnic nations are politicized ethnic communities whose spokesmen demand control over what they define as their territorial homeland. Such aspirations can eventually lead to ethnic violence and disintegration of multiethnic states. Based on this statement, one can argue that multiethnicity by itself is less likely to be in a causal relationship with ethnic violence and disintegration. But if politicization and creation of ethnic nations within multiethnic states are present, then most likely will be in a causal relation with ethnic violence and disintegration. This is the reason why the conditions that facilitate such politicizations will be explored in this study.

Domestic explanations

The effectiveness of states in regulating ethnic conflict The effectiveness of states in regulating ethnic conflict can be gauged through the study of methods used in particular periods to eliminate or manage differences between ethnic groups. A taximony of the macropolitical forms of ethnic conflict regulation, developed by McGarry and O'Leary (1993), could be used as a base for such a study. According to them, eight distinct macromethods of ethnic conflict regulation can be distinguished: (1) genocide, (2) forced mass-population transfers, (3) partition and/or secession (self-determination), (4) integration and/or assimilation as a method of eliminating differences, (5) hegemonic control, (6) arbitration (third-party intervention), (7) cantonisation and/or federalization, and (8) consociationalism or power-sharing as a method of managing differences.

It is necessary to mention that there is no single formula of state formation that can protect any particular multiethnic society from ethnic violence. In summarizing the findings of a study on ethnic conflicts, Connor (1994) reports that no particular classification of multiethnic states has proven immune to the fissiparous impact of ethnicity: authoritarian and democratic; federative and unitary; Asian, African, American, and European states have all been afflicted. Forms of government and geography have clearly not been determinative.

The impact of ethnic group politics and ethnic mobilization on state stability To study ethnic politics and mobilization, an additional specific framework is needed. Five major variants of ethnic politics will be used in this model. The same variations of ethnic politics have been used by Bugajski (1994) in his comparative studies of ethnic politics in Eastern and Central Europe and include (a) cultural revivalism, (b) political autonomism, (c)

31

territorial self-determinism, (d) separatism, and (e) irredentism. In addition, in studying ethnic mobilization I will use several critical factors identified by Esman (1994) as political opportunity structure, leadership, ideology, organization, goals, resources, strategies, and tactics.

Since some of the concepts of ethnic group policies are critical for understanding ethnic conflict, more detailed definitions are given from various perspectives. For example Hall (1979) lists and defines four kinds of ethnic autonomy: nationalism, secessionism, irredentism, and separatism. Nationalism for Hall means united and systematic political action by people or the state to achieve or maintain self-determination in the international order. He indicates further that ethnic efforts to seek autonomy outside the bounds of specific states with a view toward establishing a state centered on ethnicity may also be regarded as ethnic nationalism or separatism, and that this form of ethnic nationalism may have regional, religious, and varied political implications.

Secession is generally associated with a region that severs its ties to a union, and whether the secession is ethnically based depends upon the ethnic composition of the region breaking away. Irredentism advocates the recovery of land or territory once held by a state, or the annexation of a geographic area historically or culturally related to it. Hall recognizes the existence of ethnic irredentism when a specific ethnic group in one state proposes to, or actually does, occupy land in the legal possession of another state because of historical or cultural claims to the territory. Both ethnic irredentism and ethnic secessionism, according to him, are based on historical and cultural claims.

In defining separatism Hall observes that this form is frequently applied to movements seeking complete political independence from an existing state, and that applying the term separatism to such movements does not clearly differentiate it from nationalism and its subcategories, such as secessionism or irredentism. So, he underlined the differences:

> Nationalism involves social action geared to bring about national self-determination or large-scale social change within a state; separatism tends to emerge as an expression of a group's dissatisfaction with its lack of meaningful control over material and status resources. Unlike nationalism, separatism usually does not seek pervasive change in the international system. Rather, it is confined to ethnic action geared to enhance cultural, linguistic, religious, geographical, and economic autonomy within specific states. In this sense, separatism is a subcategory of nationalism insofar as it promotes ethnic autonomy within states, as opposed to the establishment or maintenance of national self-determination. (pp. xxi-xxiii)

McCord and McCord (in Hall, 1977) attempt to define separatist movements in more detail. They observe that separatist movements seem to emerge when one or a combination of eight variables characterize a particular situation:

First, separatist movements arise when some group has a differential access to power at the political-economic center of the state;

Second, uneven economic development that encourages the population of some regions to aspire to the affluence enjoyed by others can also play a role in some separatist movements;

Third, a separatist movement may arise if a group that has been only partially assimilated into the mainstream or dominant society finds its traditional culture dying;

Fourth, the emergence of a separatist movement requires leadership that can mobilize a population behind the cause. At times, the cause may have its roots in mythic rather than objective reality;

Fifth, successful separatist movements must create the belief that the very survival of the group requires a radical solution, and that no other alternative exists (have been exhausted);

Sixth, when a tradition of hatred has been nourished for centuries, and has been complemented by divisive religious, social, economic, political, or ethnic lines, separatism blossoms;

Seventh, at an abstract, speculative level, one could hypothesize that the relationship between the direction of economic growth and the legitimacy granted to those in power is positive;

Eighth, if a political center arrogates to itself the greatest part of political power, but allows some voices of discontent from ethnic groups, then the probability that a cry for separatism will be raised increases. (p. 433)

For Williams (1982), national separatism is a political process and, like other political processes, may be understood in terms of the factors and conditions that initiate it and subsequently determine its course of development. These may be identified as the social and environmental conditions and the integrative capabilities of the subunit in relation to the political system as a whole. According to the author, social factors include (a) the condition of the state

33

before the beginning of the secessionist movements; (b) the ethnic composition and distribution of the population; (c) the strength, mode, and agencies of resistance to secession; (d) the economic relationship of the subunit to the larger system; (e) the extent to which the subunit itself could be regarded objectively as a separate community; and, finally, (f) the exact nature of the separatist movement and the extent of its support. Williams further observes that, while ethnic, cultural, and linguistic homogeneity are no longer believed to be essential to maintaining a stable political community, they are more important for a successful secession. In his view, environmental conditions include the territorial definition and size of the separatist subunit and its location in relation to the territory of the existing state.

Hall (1979) suggests, in the table below, generalized definitions of microvariables frequently discussed in the analysis of ethnic autonomy. These variables may be used to explore how they may be associated with ethnic behavior aimed at autonomy.

The Microvariables

Culture: Attitudes, beliefs, norms, values, aesthetics, and lifestyles of a group or nation; its knowledge, actions, and material objects.

Economy: Systematic organization, production, management, and distribution of material and status values.

Ethnicity: Characteristics of internally- and externally- defined groups who behave and are regarded as a distinctive social entity.

Geography: Territory and boundary identified with or designated to specific ethnic-cultural or national groups; spatial limits of a political entity.

History: The construction or reconstruction of a nation's past from an ethnic perspective; the differences among ethnic groups' pasts in relationship to a natural history, especially between superordinate and subordinate groups.

Language: Oral/written communication of a group's systematized values, beliefs, norms, and knowledge among its members.

34

Patterns of domination:	Legitimate and illegitimate superordination; techniques and mechanisms of gaining and perpetuating superordination; to exercise transcendent authority in a social system or possess veto power in it.
Religion:	Attitudes and behavior caused by a group's belief in its relationship with the super-natural. (p. xxv)

Hall explains that domination and the patterns in which it is achieved are the most important variables associated with ethnic action aimed at autonomy, and that the other seven variables in themselves are neutral; they become active agents only insofar as they interact with patterns of domination. On the other hand, the misuse of power, the desire to dominate, the urge to control, the creation of 'us' against 'them' dichotomies where one or more variables are used to bring about the hegemony of one group over another - that is what fosters conflict.

The level of politicization of ethnic groups and potential for ethnic violence and disintegration can be identified by studying ethnic policies and the ability of governments to accommodate such policies.

Perceptual explanations - history and origin of national identity and nation-building processes, and history and origin of ethnic groups' identities and ethnocentrism

Perceptions of a people's identity play an important role in multiethnic societies. Whether one feels that he or she belongs to one nation, ethnonation or ethnic group is important in understanding potential sources of national cohesion or disintegration.

The conceptual framework that I will use to address questions of national identity and nation-building processes, and ethnic group identity and ethnocentrism, will be based on theories of nations, nation-states, nationalism and ethnonationalism. I will use concepts developed by Hans Kohn, Leonard Tivey, Anthony D. Smith, Benedict Anderson, John Breuilly, Hugh Seton-Watson, and Colin H. Williams.

Nation According to Riggs (1985), a nation is a group of people who feel themselves to be a community bound together by ties of history, culture, and common ancestry. For him, nations have objective characteristics that may include a territory, a language, a religion, or common descent, and subjective characteristics, essentially a people's awareness of its nationality and the affection for it. In the last resort, a nation is the supreme loyalty for people who are prepared to die for it.

Another view by Tivey (1981), states that what was invented in the early nineteenth century was an ideology of the nation - the belief that nations were the natural and only true political units, the foundations on which states, governments, and their policies should depend. He uses the claims of nationalists to assert that:

(1) The nation is a natural unit of society: it is inherent and not imposed or artificial. Nor is it really something chosen or voluntary, for though it may admit some new recruits, they are assimilated to an existing body.

(2) Members of the nation have a great deal in common: there is a form of homogeneity that (unlike citizenship) is not merely formal or legal. The foundations of this unit lie both in shared interests and in shared experiences, recounted in history and embodied in such things as literature, music, sport, cooking, customs and morality. Even religion may take on distinctive national forms.

(3) Each nation needs its own polity, for otherwise it will not be able to realize the fruits of its character and culture - it will be oppressed. In practice the required polity is usually an independent sovereign state, though there are occasional examples where autonomy or home rule has sufficed.

(4) All states, of course, control defined territories, but it is really the nation that has an inalienable right to its proper territory or homeland wherein to dwell.

(5) A nation should feel self-confident: it needs prestige and success, and to be respected by others. It needs to stand well in the world. (pp. 5-6)

Tivey further notes that these claims of nationalists represent an ideal type. They are nowhere, however, met in full.

Smith (1983) defines the nation as a large, vertically integrated and territorially mobile group featuring common citizenship rights and collective sentiment together with one (or more) common characteristic(s) that differentiate its members from those of similar groups with whom they stand in relations of alliance or conflict.

Smith also identifies two major perspectives on nation. Roughly, *statists* define the nation as a territorial-political unit; *ethnicists* see the nation as a large, politicized ethnic group, defined by common culture and alleged descent. The definition of nation is given by him in the broad ethnicist sense as a group with seven features:

(1) Cultural differentia (i.e., the 'similarity-dissimilarity' pattern; members are alike in respects to which they differ from nonmembers);

(2) Territorial contiguity with free mobility throughout;

(3) A relatively large scale (and population);

(4) External political relations of conflict and alliance with similar groups;

(5) Considerable group sentiment and loyalty;

(6) Direct membership with equal citizenship rights;

(7) Vertical economic integration around a common system of labor. (p. 186)

Smith (1991) also identifies a Western and non-Western concept of the nation. A Western, or *civic,* model of the nation is, in the first place, a predominantly spatial or territorial conception. According to this view, nations must possess compact, well-defined territories. Commenting further, the author writes:

It is, and must be, the historic land, the homeland, the cradle of our people, even where it is not the land of ultimate origin. A historical land is one where terrain and people have exerted mutual, and beneficial, influence over several generations. The homeland becomes a repository of historic memories and associations, the place where 'our' sage, saints and heroes lived, worked, prayed and fought. All this makes the homeland unique. Its rivers, coasts, lakes, mountains and cities become sacred - places of veneration and exaltation whose inner meanings can be fathomed only by the initiated, that is, the self-aware members of the nation. National territory must become self-sufficient. Autarchy is as much a defense of sacred homelands as of economic interests. (pp. 9-10)

This civic model contains another important feature. Smith continues:

A second element is the idea of a *patria*, a community of laws and institutions with a single political will. Concurrent with the growth of

37

a sense of legal and political community one may trace a sense of legal equality among the members of the community. Its full expression is the various kinds of 'citizenship' that sociologists have enumerated, including civil and legal rights, political rights and duties, and socio-economic rights. Here it is legal and political rights that the Western conception considers integral to its model of a nation. (p.10)

Finally, according to Smith:

> The legal equality of members of a political community in its demarcated homeland was felt to presuppose a measure of common values and traditions among the population, or at any rate its 'core' community. In other words, nations must have a measure of common culture and civic ideology, a set of common understandings and aspirations, sentiments and ideas, that bind the population together in their homeland. The task of ensuring a common public, mass culture has been handed over to the agencies of popular socialization, notably the public system of education and the mass media. In the Western model of national identity, nations were seen as cultural communities, whose members were united, if not made homogeneous, by common historical memories, myths, symbols and traditions. (pp.10-11)

In short, historic territory, legal-political community, legal-political equality of members, and common civic culture and ideology - these are the components of the standard, Western model of the nation.

At the same time that these concepts arose, a rather different model of the nation sprang up outside the West, in Eastern Europe and Asia. Smith termed this non-Western model an *ethnic* conception of the nation. He notes that its distinguishing feature is in the emphasis on a community of birth and native culture, while the Western concept specifies that an individual has to belong to some nation, but can choose the one he or she prefers. This ethnic model also has a number of facets, defined by Smith as:

> First, obviously, is the stress on descent - or rather, presumed descent - rather than territory. The nation is seen as a fictive super-family, and it boasts pedigrees and genealogies to back up its claims, often tracked down by native intellectuals, particularly in the East European and Middle Eastern countries. The point here is that, in this conception, the nation can trace its roots to an imputed common ancestry and that therefore its members are brothers and sisters, or at least cousins, differentiated by family ties from outsiders. (p.12)

38

A strong popular element in the ethnic conception of the nation can be explained by the concept of family ties. Again, Smith explains:

> People figure in the Western model too, but there they are seen as a political community subject to common laws and institutions. In the ethnic model the people, even where they are not actually mobilized for political action, nevertheless provide the object of nationalist aspirations and the final rhetorical court of appeal. Leaders can justify their action and unite disparate classes and groups only through an appeal to the 'will of the people', and this makes the ethnic concept more obviously inter-class and populist in tone, even when the intelligentsia has little intention of summoning the masses into the political arena. Popular mobilization, therefore, plays an important moral and rhetorical, if not an actual, role in the ethnic conception. (p.12)

He observes that the place of law in the Western civic model is taken by vernacular culture, usually languages and customs, in the ethnic model, and comments further:

> That is why lexicographers, philologists and folklorists have played a central role in the early nationalism of eastern Europe and Asia. Their linguistic and ethnographic research into the past and present culture of the 'folk' provided the materials for a blueprint of the 'nation-to-be' even here specific linguistic revivals failed. By creating a widespread awareness of the myths, history and linguistic traditions of the community, they succeeded in substantiating and crystallizing the idea of an ethnic nation in the minds of most members, even when, as in Ireland and Norway, the ancient languages declined. (p.12)

In short, genealogy and presumed descent ties, popular mobilization, vernacular languages, customs, and traditions: these are the elements of an alternative, ethnic conception of the nation, one that mirrors the very different route of "nation-formation" travelled by many communities in Eastern Europe and Asia, and one that has constituted a dynamic political challenge.

Smith's final arguments are that every nationalism contains civic and ethnic elements in varying degrees and forms. Nevertheless, it is important to identify in specific multiethnic states which elements have been used in the process of political institutionalization of the nation-state. In socialist countries, for example, the official ideology could be closer to the civic concept, while the real political institutionalization is closer to the ethnic concept. Such distortions may create conditions for ethnic violence and disintegration.

Anderson (1991) proposes the following definition of the nation:

It is an imagined political community - and imagined as both inherently limited and sovereign.

It is imagined because the members of even the smallest nation will never know most of their fellow-members, meet them, or even hear of them, yet in the minds of each lives the image of their communion. ... In fact, all communities larger than primordial villages of face-to-face contact (and perhaps even these) are imagined. ...

The nation is imagined as limited because even the largest of them, encompassing perhaps a billion living human beings, has finite, if elastic, boundaries, beyond which lie other nations. ...

It is imagined as sovereign because the concept was born in an age in which Enlightenment and Revolution were destroying the legitimacy of the divinely-ordained, hierarchical dynastic realm. ... The gage and emblem of the freedom is the sovereign state.

Finally it is imagined as a community, because, regardless of the actual inequality and exploitation that may prevail in each, the nation is always conceived as a deep, horizontal comradeship. Ultimately it is this fraternity that makes it possible, over the past two centuries, for so many millions of people, not so much to kill, as willingly to die for such limited imaginings.

These deaths bring us abruptly face to face with the central problem posed by nationalism: What makes the shrunken imaginings of recent history (scarcely more than two centuries) generate such colossal sacrifices? I believe that the beginning of an answer lies in the cultural roots of nationalism. (pp. 5-7)

Anderson's argument that the nation is an imagined political community acknowledges the potential for distortion. Any imagined phenomena could be manipulated and used for different purposes. Ideologies, doctrines, and virtually constructed realities can be used in shaping one's mind and one's loyalty to either civic nation or ethnonation.

From this listing of theories of nations, one can see that different authors use different variables to define nation. In order to further facilitate analysis of nations and nation-building, I created a table (table 3.1) incorporating all the variables mentioned above and have identified which of these variables are associated with each of these theories.

Table 3.1
Theories of nation

Defining features variables	Riggs	Tivey	Smith Civic	Smith Ethnic	Anderson
Group of people	*	*			
Community bound	*				
History	*	*		*	
Common culture	*	*	*	*	
Common ancestry	*	*		*	
Territory	*	*	*		
Language	*			*	
Religion	*				
Awareness of nationality	*				
Affection	*				
Supreme loyalty	*	*			
Natural unit of society		*			
Inherent		*			
Homogeneity		*			
Shared interest		*			
Shared experience		*			
Literature		*			
Music		*			
Sport		*			
Cooking		*			

Customs		*		*	
Morality		*			
Polity		*			
Self-confidence		*			
Cradle			*		
Historic land			*		
Homeland			*		
Sages			*		
Saints			*		
Heroes			*		
Rivers			*		
Lakes			*		
Coasts			*		
Mountains			*		
Cities			*		
Sacred places			*		
Self-sufficient Territory			*		
Legal and political community			*		
Legal equality			*		
Civil and legal rights			*		
Political rights and duties			*		
Socio-economic rights			*		

Cultural community			*		
Memories			*		
Myths			*	*	
Symbols			*		
Traditions			*	*	
Choice to join or not			*		
Community of birth				*	
Native culture				*	
Super-family				*	
Popular mobilization				*	
Imagined community					*
Willing to die					*
Horizontal comradeship					*

This table has been created just for analytical purposes. It shows that when people speak about the nation, it does not always include the same, or even similar, phenomena. From the list of variables used in different theories, one can see that the concept of nation differs significantly among them. The small amount of overlap is striking evidence which supports the claim of this chapter that a need exists first to deal with the concept itself. It is also necessary to emphasize that these theories present ideal types, not true depictions of reality.

Nationalism The first full manifestation of modern nationalism, according to Kohn (1965), occurred in seventeenth-century England. In his words, 'For the first time the authoritarian tradition on which the Church and the State had rested was challenged by the seventeenth century English Revolutions in the name of the liberty of man' (p. 16). The English, American, and French Revolutions of 1688, 1776, and 1789, respectively, started a new era, one of nations and nation-states. Also, there are competing points of view that variously credit the Peace of Westphalia in 1648 and Louis XIV (1638-1715) as being the origins of the modern nation-state.

Riggs (1985) views nationalism as both an ideology and a form of behavior. The ideology of nationalism builds on people's awareness of a nation (national self-consciousness) to give both a set of attitudes and a program of action. These can be cultural, economic, or political. Since 'nation' can be defined in 'ethnic', 'social', or 'official' senses, so can nationalism take these forms also. Riggs emphasizes that nationalism seeks to defend and promote the interests of the nation. The political aspect of nationalism is seen most clearly in the demand for 'national self-determination' or 'home-rule.' For states, 'official nationalism' means patriotism and the defense of 'national sovereignty' in international relations, and all types of nationalism seek a political expression for the nation, most strongly in independent statehood.

Kohn (1965) observes that nationalism has been one of the determining forces in modern history. For him it originated in eighteenth-century Western Europe, spreading all over Europe in the nineteenth century to become a worldwide movement in the twentieth century. In his opinion, nationalism is a historical phenomenon and is thus determined by the political ideas and social structure of the various lands where it takes root. Nationalism is a state of mind in which the supreme loyalty of the individual is felt to be due the nation-state. Formerly, a man's loyalty was due not to the nation-state but to other differing forms of social authority, political organization, and ideological cohesion such as the tribe or clan, the city-state or feudal lord, the dynastic state, the church or religious group.

According to Hayes (in Symmons-Symonolewicz, 1986, pp. 25-26), the term nationalism may refer to (a) the actual historical process of establishing nationalities as political units, (b) a political philosophy of the nation-state, (c) a popular movement or activities of political parties representing nationalist orientation, or (d) a condition of mind among the members of a nationality.

Another definition of the term by Breully (1982) states that nationalism is used to refer to political movements seeking or exercising state power and justifying such actions with a nationalist argument. A nationalist argument is a political doctrine built upon three basic assertions:

(1) There exists a nation with an explicit and peculiar character;

(2) The interests and values of this nation take priority over all other interests and values;

(3) The nation must be as independent as possible. This usually requires at least the attainment of political sovereignty. (p. 3)

44

In an effort to group theories of nationalism, Breuilly also identifies the following approaches to theories of nationalism:

(1) The nationalist approach. This approach assumes that nationalism is an expression of the nation. The nation desires independence and the nationalists simply articulate and try to realize that desire.

(2) The communications approach. This approach sees the nation in terms of a developed system of internal communications, that create a sense of common identity. However, this approach emphasizes that the intensified communication between individuals and groups can as often lead to an increase in internal conflict as to an increase in solidarity. It is argued that the structure of communications provides no direct indication as to the structure of political conflict, and it is on the latter that one must concentrate.

(3) The Marxist approach. The Marxist approach focuses upon internal class conflict in a particular society. It can regard a nationalist movement as the work and expression of a single class, with relatively little involvement by other classes. It can regard nationalism in terms of a set of class alliances in which each class has its own rational interest. It can also regard nationalism as representing the interests of a particular class but inducing other classes to support that nationalism.

(4) The psychological and functional approaches. There are many variations upon the psychological approach. According to this approach the whole point of nationalism is its insistence on the importance of a special cultural group identity (like an ethnic group) as the bedrock of political claims and action. It emphasizes that a major concern of modern social thought is the problem of community, of how common identity and sentiments of solidarity can be created in the face of impersonal, abstract, 'rational' relationships based on calculations, and that within this body of thought a contrast is frequently drawn between warm, intimate, spontaneous relationships supposedly characteristic of community, and cold, distant, reflective relationships supposedly characteristic of society. Nationalism as an ideology can be regarded as a way of bridging these differences.

The functional approach is closely related to the psychological one. The functionalist sociology often works with a dichotomy between tradition and modernity, community and society, and tends to perceive rapid change as a breakdown of the relationships and values of the first of these, leading to the establishment of relationships and values characteristic of the second. A major implication is that rapid change precipitates a breakdown of traditional identity, and the coming of modernity points to the shape a new identity can take (Breuilly, 1982, pp. 18-36).

Smith (1983) elaborates on *ethnocentric* versus *polycentric* nationalism. For an ethnocentric nationalist, both power and value inhere in his cultural group, which is the vessel of wisdom, beauty, holiness, culture; hence, power automatically belongs as an attribute to that group. Polycentric nationalism, by contrast, resembles the dialogue of many actors on a common stage. As the term implies, this kind of nationalism starts from the premise that there are many centers of real power; other groups do have valuable and genuinely noble ideas and institutions that others would do well to borrow or adapt, or at least accept them.

Seton-Watson (1977) describes nationalism as having two basic meanings: (1) A doctrine about the character, interests, rights and duties of nations; and (2) an organized political movement designed to further the alleged aims and interests of nations such as independence-creation of a sovereign state, national unity, and nation-building within the independent state. The three major aims of nationalism therefore are independence, union, and nation-building.

Since the objective of this chapter is to define major concepts that can be used later for analysis of particular cases, such as Yugoslavia, I want to underline the forms of nationalism used in this study. They are (a) official or state nationalism that leads to nation-building and unification within the existing state boundaries; (b) nationalism that leads to independence, such as liberation movements; and (c) ethno-nationalism driven by the idea of self-determination that leads to dissolution of existing states and creation of new sovereign states. It is possible to derive more forms of nationalism from these theories of nationalism, but for the purpose of this work , three are adequate.

Nation-state Tivey (1981) provides the following definition of a nation-state:

> A nation-state is commonly defined as a polity of homogeneous people who share the same culture and the same language, and who are governed by some of their own members, who serve their interests. If we ask when such a state of affairs came into being, we should say, at no time. There is no people in the world that shares such a homogeneity, where there are no regional or cultural differences, where all speak the same language or share the same linguistic usage and where the rulers do not differ in rank or wealth or education from the ruled. Actual nation-states rather approximate to an ideal type than mirror it, and do so in very different degrees. (p. 13)

In an effort to explain national separatism, Williams (1982) gives the following definition of a nation-state:

A nation state is a political community with three major properties or capabilities of integration. These are, first, that it is able to exercise a monopoly of political authority and legitimate force within its territory; second, that it has a government which is a decision-making center able to determine or significantly influence the allocation of resources in the society; and third, that it operates as a focus for political identification, loyalty and support amongst the population. These capabilities may be described as coercive, instrumental and identive. (p. 300)

Another definition by Smith (1983) presents the nation-state as a nation with de facto territorial sovereignty.

Though short, his definition tells the most about the nation-state. Nonetheless, I would like to extend this definition by adding some of the statements of Kis (1989), who defines the state as follows:

(1) A state must have a territory to call its own;

(2) A state must have a permanent population;

(3) A state must have a government and a system of laws by which it maintains control over its territory and population; and

(4) The government must have the capacity or competence to enter into relations with other states on equal terms. (pp. 14-15)

The nation-state can thus be defined as a state with a nation that has a permanent population living in a particular territory, has its own government, and is recognized as sovereign by the international community.

Ethnic group, ethnocentrism and ethnicity According to Riggs (1985), ethnic group and ethnocentrism are comparable to nation and nationalism. The difference between them is that an ethnic group is more narrowly defined than nation, and ethnocentrism is more rooted in social psychology than is nationalism, which has explicitly ideological and political dimensions. In addition, ethnic groups are generally differentiated from nations on several dimensions: they are usually smaller; they are more clearly based on a common ancestry; and they are more pervasive in human history, while nations are perhaps specific to time and place. Also, ethnic groups are essentially exclusive or ascriptive, meaning that membership in such groups is confined to those who share certain inborn attributes; nations, on the other hand, are more inclusive and are culturally or politically defined.

For Riggs ethnocentric is basically a psychological term, although it is also used in the study of society and politics. It can be related to nationalism and racism, but its focus is strictly on the individual's relationship with an ethnic group rather than with a nation or a race. It is essentially concerned with an individual's psychological bias toward his or her ethnic group, and against other ethnic groups. The intensity of ethnocentric attitudes and behavior varies from mild and peaceful to belligerent and megalomaniac.

Riggs interprets ethnicity as the state of being ethnic, or belonging to an ethnic group. For him it is a more neutral term than ethnocentrism which, as we have seen, denotes prejudicial attitudes favoring one ethnic group and rejecting others. He adds that, while some nations may be called ethnic nations, there are ethnic groups who do not claim to be nations, and that the difference may be found in the character of ethnic politics. While nationalism focuses on national self-determination, or home rule in a national territory, ethnic politics, in contrast, is largely concerned with the protection of rights for members of the group within the existing state, with no claim for a territorial homeland. Riggs notes that these distinctions are not made by all scholars.

Definitions of nation and nationalism from one side and of ethnic group and ethnocentrism (ethnonationalism) from the other side are important for an analytical framework. Based on these definitions, one can argue about the right for self-determination and creation of new nation-states.

International explanations

Changes in the world order and the role of the United Nations (the League of Nations) in regulating intrastate ethnic conflicts In this analysis ethnic conflict is compared as a source of either national cohesion or disintegration with the different international orders since 1918. The world orders will be differentiated based on the concepts of peace and security developed and institutions and policies created to implement it.

Based on these characteristics it is possible to differentiate (1) the world order created at the end of the First World War based on the compromised principle of self-determination and a collective security system with universal veto power in the League of Nations. Its major objective was to protect states against aggression by other states; (2) the world order created at the end of the Second World War based on the power balancing that led to the Cold War and the United Nations security system with limited veto power, restricted to the permanent members of the Security Council. It had the primary objective to provide security and territorial integrity to independent and sovereign nation-states; and (3) the world order in the aftermath of the Cold War with the emerging United Nations collective security system, which is expected to reflect universal values such as democracy, self-determination, human rights guarantees, and nonviolence. The new security system of the United Nations is also expected to provide security to subnational entities, and as such to play an important role in intrastate conflicts.

Development of the principles of self-determination vs. territorial integrity and sovereignty of existing states A definition of the principle of self-determination should be the start-line of any analysis of world order, concepts of peace and security, and institutions and policies created to protect the established systems. As such, more elaboration of this principle is needed. Although the expression 'self-determination of nations' can be traced to 1865, it did not receive great attention until its endorsement by a number of world-renowned statesmen during the World War I era (Connor, 1994).

For the purpose of my study the question of self-determination is defined as it was elaborated at the end of World War I. At that time Woodrow Wilson's idea of self-determination was dominant and was critical for the period of history when many new nation-states were created. Pomerance (1982) describes self-determination, as conceived by Wilson, as an imprecise amalgam of several strands of thought, some long associated in his mind with the notion of self-government, others newly hatched as a result of wartime developments, but all imbued with a general spirit of democracy (consent of the governed). Elaborating further, he states:

> Wilson had long held that every people had the right to select its own form of government - an idea that might be termed internal self-determination. Moreover, if consent was to be given continuously, rather than as a one-time exercise, the form of government chosen would probably have to be democratic. Later, in the context of the war, 'consent of governed' came to subsume 'external' self-determination as well: the right of every people to choose the sovereignty under which they live, to be free of alien masters, and not to be handed about from sovereignty to sovereignty as if they were property. Finally, the exigencies of the European war also led to the close linking of 'self-determination' with the principle of nationalities, so that the 'self' which was to determine its own fate began, more and more, to assume an ethnographic character. This development was least in accord with Wilson's own thought, which strongly preferred the atomistic Anglo-American view of the nation as a community of organization, of life, and of tradition to the German collectivist concept of the 'Volk' as a community of blood and of origin. Geographically, the applicability of the self-determination principle was not, in Wilson's mind, confined to Europe. Asian and African people too might, after proper tutelage, become fit for self-government. (pp. 1-2)

49

The first major testing ground for this package of ideas took place at the Versailles Peace Conference. The major question was, Who is the 'self' to whom the right of self-determination attaches? At Paris, it was queried whether the unit contemplated by Wilson was 'a race, a territorial area, or a community' but the question is, in fact, far more complex. For Pomerance, selection of any one of these units requires further decisions with respect to delimitation, exclusion, and inclusion. For example, What are the boundaries of the area? Who are its inhabitants? Who are the members of the race or the community? He argues that the territorial and ethnic criteria are not neatly separable; they are, rather, inextricably interwoven, and it is necessary to determine which population belongs to which area. The necessity of defining the 'self' who is to exercise self-determination lies at the heart of what is probably the most basic dilemma in the matter of self-determination. Further, notes the author, recognition of the rights of one's self entails a denial of the rights of a competing 'self.' For, in essence, every demand for self-determination involves some countervailing claim or claims.

Other questions plagued Wilson and his fellow peacemakers at Versailles and beyond. How, for example, were the wishes of the 'self' to be determined? Must plebiscites be conducted in all cases, or were other methods sometimes permissible or preferable? Could reliance be placed on expert commissions or on the views of a body claiming to represent the people concerned? It may be recalled that Wilson recognized the Masaryk-Benes committee as the representative of the people of Czechoslovakia. Moreover, none of the secession states were established by plebiscite. That tool was reserved for certain disputed border areas only.

Pomerance observes that, according to Wilson, other principles needed to be considered in the peacemaking, and these sometimes seemed to clash with the requirements of self-determination. Such principles included access to the seas and traditional international law - such as the sanctity of treaties. Still other considerations, of an economic, strategic, and historic nature, could be ignored, it was felt, only at great peril. In the face of the innumerable theoretical and practical difficulties surrounding universal implementation of the principle of self-determination, it is hardly surprising that the peacemakers at Versailles, and especially Wilson, were subsequently charged with the betrayal of the principle and the application of double standards. They did not and could not satisfy the desires of every claimant waving the flag of self-determination. Pomerance also elaborates on external self-determination and internal self-determination. In theory, it is possible to distinguish between external self-determination - the act by which a people determines its future international status and liberates itself from alien rule, and internal self-determination - the selection of the desired system of government.

In contrast to Wilson's perceptions and concept of self-determination, Lenin had a different perception of the problem of self-determination, as discussed in an earlier chapter. Since Lenin conceived of self-determination in purely negative terms, he was therefore convinced that the best way to avoid or to dissipate a grass-roots demand for independence was to promise right of self-determination to groups with such demands and to eliminate this option in practice through the introduction of democratic centralism as the major principle of decision making in the Communist Party and the society.

It is also necessary to look at the question of self-determination from the perspective of peaceful separation and disintegration of existing states. Mayall (1990) concludes that not many positive examples are found in history. The only relatively peaceful modern secessions were Norway from Sweden in 1905 and the Irish Free State from the United Kingdom in 1921. More recently there is the case of Czechoslovakia, which has separated into two states.

The international order between the two world wars and during the Cold War was developed based on the assumption that the nation-states created at the end of the First World War were the pillars of the world order. Any problem or conflict within the boundary of nation-states was considered an internal matter of the sovereign state rather than a matter for the international community. During the Cold War, however, and particularly in its aftermath, the concept of nation-states was challenged by subnational entities such as ethnic groups. Some old nation-states such as Yugoslavia were dissolved and new states were created and recognized by the international community. Yet, again, as was the case at the end of the First World War, the concept of self-determination has been compromised, with some ethnic groups being awarded the right to create their own states while denying the same right to others. At the same time, the role of the United Nations has changed during these processes, with more emphasis on intervention and enforcement within the boundaries of nation-states. The new directions were set out in Boutros Boutros-Ghali's *An Agenda for Peace* (1992), and the transformation of the United Nations and its policies is now under way, having been forced to it by the increased ethnic violence in Yugoslavia and other regions in the world.

Applying the model to the case of Yugoslavia

Recent events in Yugoslavia and in the world in general have revealed the complexity of current societies burdened with historic conflicts and animosities. Expectations that after the Cold War era the world would enter a period of peaceful cooperation and integration were diminished as the world community saw conflicts develop in Yugoslavia and other multiethnic states. With the new environment after the Cold War, longstanding historic conflicts in some regions have resurfaced and resulted in violence. Yugoslavia, as already mentioned, represents one of the worst cases in the 1990s.

In dealing with ethnic violence, one should first try to reveal the nature of the conflicts and investigate different means that might help troubled countries and regions to deal with them. In the case of Yugoslavia, one can use the model elaborated in this chapter to look at two parallel processes, one of the state, official, and party nationalism and nation-building, and the other of ethnonationalism and self-determination. These processes can also be called processes of national integration and national disintegration. In analyzing the historical development of a nation such as Yugoslavia, one finds that the development went through periods of peace and stability as well as periods of violence and wars.

There are many entry points for an analysis of Yugoslav disintegration. For the purpose of this study it makes sense to begin with the creation of Yugoslavia in 1918. This event was marked by a compromise of Woodrow Wilson's principle of self-determination that proclaimed the right of every nation to create its own nation-state. In part this was due to the poorly defined concept of nation as it was more than 70 years ago. Subsequently, in the application of a vaguely defined concept of nation to the concept of self-determination, it was not clear whether the sovereign 'self' belongs exclusively to a 'nation.' Yugoslavia, as a monarchy, and then as Tito's socialist state, tried to build a Yugoslav nation and preserve the integrity of an always challenged nation-state. All kinds of methods have been used to achieve this objective, among them populist ideologies, suppression, and coercion. Existing theories of the meaning of nation should help to analyze the nature of the Yugoslav nation and to find whether a Yugoslav nation ever existed, and if so, in what form.

The analysis of ethnic composition and the cleavages among different ethnic groups easily reveal possible roots of disintegration and violence. Analysis of ethnic group politics and ethnic mobilizations could also help to identify the objectives of Croats, Moslems, Serbs, and other ethnic groups. For example, questions might include, What form of state did they ask for? What kind of ethnic autonomy did they ask for? Was this autonomy within the existing states, secessionism, or irredentism? I believe that all these forms are to be found in different periods and in different Balkan regions. An analysis of the effectiveness of the Yugoslav government and administrative state in regulating ethnic conflict in certain periods should identify the capacity of particular methods and policies to eliminate or manage differences among ethnic groups. Analysis of the international orders, concepts, principles, and institutions in different periods facilitate understanding and identify the nature of relationships between certain international contexts and intrastate ethnic conflict and violence.

In the process of analyzing the sources of national cohesion and disintegration, it is possible to test my arguments. The role of Yugoslav worker self-management is explored regarding its contribution to ethnic violence and national disintegration. The perceptual aspect of the ideology of self-management regarding national cohesion is elaborated parallel with political and administrative institutions and government regulatory policies of ethnic conflict. It is explained how institutionalization of self-management led to the decentralization of Yugoslavia, which subsequently led to the gradual development of ethnonationalism and ultimately, in the period of transition, to a multiparty democracy, to self-determination, and to secession of ethnonational groups. The role of the international community is analyzed as the source of national cohesion and disintegration. Finally an effort is made to identify international conditions that are likely to generate ethnic violence and disintegration in already ethnically divided countries.

Upon identification and analysis of these phenomena, one might next try to identify strategies, policies, and actions that could deal with consequences and the devastating effects of ethno-nationalism in Yugoslavia. This approach could provide the strategy for promoting democratization, as recommended by Riggs (1994).

Notes

1. Hobbes considered that in the state of nature 'the life of man is solitary, poor, nasty, brutish, and short.'

2. The Lockean world view was of a state of nature characterized by 'peace, good will, mutual assistance, and preservation.'

4 Creation of Yugoslavia

The Kingdom of the Serbs, Croats, and Slovenes was created in 1918 as the nation-state of the South Slavs. In its evolution the Kingdom of the Serbs, Croats, and Slovenes (1918-1929) eventually became the Kingdom of Yugoslavia (1929-1941), then the Federal People's Republic of Yugoslavia (1943-1963), and finally the Socialist Federal Republic of Yugoslavia (1963-1991). The process of nation-building of the Yugoslav nation went through different periods of domestic and international challenge. Leadership, the state, parties, ideology, and common threat played important roles in the nation-building process. Ethnic cleavages within the nation-state originated in the different histories of Yugoslavia's ethnic groups and have persisted throughout the relatively short history of that country.

South Slav perceptions of the Yugoslav nation as a new invention overlapped with perceptions of their separate history of nationhood and statehood. Even though Yugoslavia was made up of the Serbs, Croats, Slovenes, Montenegrins, Macedonians, and Moslems, the major line of cleavage occurred between Serbs and Croats. Their shared border was also the border between different religions and civilizations. In a land gap between them for centuries lived Slavs exposed to different religions and civilizations that determined their national identities. In the twelfth century the Slavs in the gap had Bosnian identity defined by a Bosnian Church, separating them from the other Slavs, but in later periods Bosnians developed identities of Serbs, Croats, and Moslems along the religious cleavages of Greek Orthodox, Roman Catholics, and Moslems. The proximity of Serbs, Croats, and later Muslims made their relations most vulnerable to ethnic group mobilization and violence.

This study will deal with cleavages developed among them that could be regarded as a systemic independent variable. Their ethnonational identities could be regarded as perceptual independent variables developed throughout the history of Serbian, Croatian, and Moslem nationhood and statehood. The proximity of different ethnic groups inevitably sets up a systemic condition for ethnic violence. It is, however, the particular composition of variables that could trigger violence at the expense of ethnic cooperation. Proximity and ethnic nationalism, in the absence of national unity and civic society, were to be the conditions for disaster.

In this chapter the objective is to explore the origins of Croatian, Serbian, and Moslem nationhood and statehood and to examine the factors that led to their integration into a single state in 1918. In later chapters I will examine the internal Yugoslav nation-building efforts and their failure to develop a nation-state that could accommodate and reconcile differences in the origins of Serbs, Croats, and Moslems.

South Slavs in the Balkans

The South Slavs are one of three branches of the Slavic peoples, the other two being the East Slavs (Russians, Ukrainians, Byelorussians) and the West Slavs (Poles, Czechs, Slovaks). The original land of the Slavic peoples is considered to be the area now occupied by the republics of Belarus and Ukraine. The South Slavs populated the Balkans in the sixth and seventh centuries (Shoemaker, 1993).

It took three to four centuries for the first South Slav state to appear in the Balkans. In the period between the tenth and the fourteenth century, the first South Slav states reached their zeniths and disappeared under the conquest of Hungarian, Austro-Hungarian, and Ottoman empires. At the end of the eighteenth and the beginning of the nineteenth century, a strong South Slav national consciousness driven by events in France and Europe appeared within the two realms. Serbian and Croatian national movements for independence and self-determination dominated the political agenda of the Balkans in the nineteenth century. These led to formation of the Kingdom of the Serbs, Croats, and Slovenes at the beginning of the twentieth century.

National movements of South Slav ethnic groups, however, had different patterns dictated by the characteristics of political, cultural, and religious environments of their neighbors, invaders, and masters. The Balkans have been a battlefield of civilizations for much of recorded history. The final schism between Eastern and Western Christianity in 1054 and the appearance of Islam in the fourteenth century greatly affected the lives of the South Slav people. Different religions, cultures, and political realms over the centuries developed different traditions, despite the fact that the mutual language remained one of the most significant indicators that they belonged to the same people.

55

During the centuries of their presence in the Balkans, different South Slav groups developed distinctive characteristics that become embedded in history and divided by natural boundaries, such as rivers (Sava, Danube, Drava, Drina and Una), mountains, and basins.

The South Slavs had been used by both Austro-Hungarians and Turks as a shield against the opposing civilization. The military frontier was populated by South Slavs, mostly Serbs who had escaped the Ottoman conquest. These Serbs and other South Slavs defended Austro-Hungary from further invasion of the Ottoman Empire (map 4.1), while 'kapetanije' frontier districts formed by Turks and populated by Serbs protected the Ottoman Empire from Austro-Hungarian intrusions.

Divided by history, conquest, religion, and culture the South Slav people cultivated different perceptions of nationhood and statehood. However, despite the differences, the consciousness of a shared fate and the idea of unification of all South Slavs into one state had existed for many centuries. In 1918, at the end of the First World War, the South Slavs finally got an opportunity to create a unified state. This state lasted for about 70 years. In 1991 ethnic conflict erupted that led to the dismemberment of Yugoslavia.

History and origin of Croatian national identity and statehood

First and only Croatian state (924-1087)

Croats, Serbs, and other South Slavs had been ruled by tribal institutions since the beginning of the tenth century (map 4.2). At the beginning of the tenth century, the Croatian ruler Tomislav succeeded in uniting the various Croatian tribes under his rule. In 924, he was crowned as king (rex) in the presence of envoys of Pope Constantine and the Byzantine Emperor Porphyrogenit. The Croatian Kingdom reached its zenith under the Tomislav rule. This period of history is looked on by Croats as the golden age of Croatia. The Croatian Kingdom succeeded in building up a large navy and achieving recognition as a military power (map 4.3). However, the Croatians' military potential led to the state's downfall. The Croatian armies and navies were engaged by foreign rulers (e.g. the popes) for their military ventures.

The last of the Croatian rulers, King Zvonimir, become virtually a military vassal of Pope Gregory VII. The King's position was not popular with the Croats. In 1087, he was killed during a rebellion at Knin and the country lapsed into discord, ending in the cessation of an independent Croatian state (Hondius, 1968; Curtis, 1992).

Map 4.1 Military Frontier

Map prepared according to Magocsi, Paul R., *Historical Atlas of East Central Europe*

Map 4.2 The South Slav tribes in the Balkans

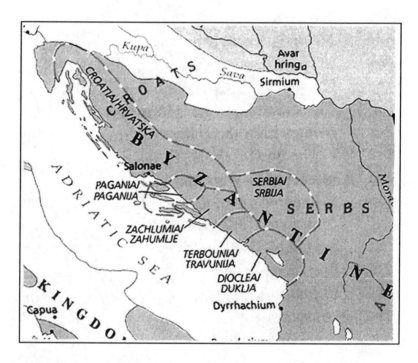

Map prepared according to Magocsi, Paul R., *Historical Atlas of East Central Europe*

Map 4.3 The first Croatian state

Map prepared according to Magocsi, Paul R., *Historical Atlas of East Central Europe*

Croatia under Hungarian rule (1095-1526)

The hereditary and feudal successors to the old Croatian tribal leaders could not agree on who among them would succeed Zvonimir. The crown was offered to a Hungarian, Ladislas Arpad, who treated his Croatian lands as conquered territory. After his death in 1095, his brother, the Hungarian King Koloman, was recognized by Croats as their overlord under unclear terms. According to Croatian interpretation, Croatia united with Hungary in a personal union, while the Magyars considered the union an incorporation by right of the sword (Hondius, 1968; Curtis, 1992).

Under the rule of the Hungarian kings, Croatia was able to retain its own political institutions. Croatia and Hungary each had its own Diet. Bills voted in the Croatian Diet had the force of law when they received royal assent without Hungarian Diet approval. They also had their own Ban (local ruler).

Despite this political autonomy, Croatia remained subjugated to the Hungarian Kingdom and later to the Austro-Hungarian Monarchy for the next nine centuries. Croatia never again regained political power beyond some local autonomy. The unclear political position of Croatia and Croats within the Hungarian Kingdom until 1526, and later the Austro-Hungarian Monarchy, was rooted in the dual perceptions (volunteer union and/or right of sword) of the very origin of the Hungarian Kingdom. This burdened the Croatians' perception of their own history. The name of Croatia never again appeared in the name of any of the Hungarian and Austro-Hungarian realms. Only in 1918 did the name Croatia appear again in the name of the Kingdom of the Serbs, Croats, and Slovenes.

Croatia under the Hapsburgs (1526-1800)

Hungarian power was broken by the Turks in the battle of Mohacs in 1526 when King Louis Jagiello died, and Hungary and Croatia remained without an overlord. The Hungarians were not able to agree on a successor. One group of Hungarian nobles placed Ferdinand of Hapsburg (1503-1564) in possession of the crown of St. Stephen, while Hungarian nationalists elected as their King John Zapolyai of Transylvania. The split within the Hungarian nobility pushed Croatians to take sides. Threatened by Turks, the Croats once again opted for a foreign protectorate. They missed the chance to elect their own king, Ban Krsto Frankopan, who was not able to gain the confidence of the Croatian Sabor (Assembly). On 1 January 1527 the Sabor elected King Ferdinand of Hapsburg as '. . . true, lawful, unchallengeable and natural King and Lord to our and this whole glorious Kingdom of Croatia' (Hondius, 1968, p. 40).

Oppressed more and more by the Hapsburgs, the Croats tried to balance their power of by offering more power to the Hungarian Diet. As a result, from 1593 and during the seventeenth century, Croatians sent delegates to the Hungarian Diet.

Political life under the Hungarian and Austro-Hungarian regimes developed a particular political culture among the Croatian people. In permanent political games played for centuries with the Hungarian and Hapsburg rulers, Croatians succeeded in maintaining their politically autonomous status as an ethnic group within the broader political realms. They were not, however, able to regain the independence they had lost in the eleventh century.

French Revolution, Napoleon War, and Croatia

The end of the eighteenth and beginning of the nineteenth century became a very important period for future Croatian nationhood and statehood. It was a period of significant change for political configuration in Europe. Nationalism, the weakening of old political powers, and the birth of new nations triggered Croatians to move toward their own nationhood and statehood.

The curious episode of Napoleon's Illyrian Provinces is illustrative of this era. As a result of the Treaties of Presburg (1805) and Schonbrunn (1809), Austria was forced to cede to France her former Venetian possessions (including Dalmatia) of Slovenia and most of Croatia. Out of these territories Napoleon shaped a new unit, the Illyrian Provinces, attached to his puppet Kingdom of Italy (map 4.4). The French tried to give a political structure and national content to the Illyrian Provinces. They sought the supposed national values of the inhabitants, the 'Illyrians,' even inventing 'national' values as they sought to create a new nation.

Upon the defeat of Napoleon in 1815, the Illyrian territories were returned to the Austrians. After 1822, however, Croatia again belonged to the Hungarians. The Magyars, in order to increase their dominance over Croatians, in 1840 and 1843 made the Magyar language compulsory for official business and education. In 1843, the use of the words Illyria, Illyrism, and Illyrian was prohibited by King Ferdinand of Hungary. In response, in 1847 the Croatian Sabor declared Croatian the official language, marking the beginning of a violent anti-Magyar campaign in Croatia.

Despite the prohibition of the Magyars, the idea for which Illyrism stood remained present within the South Slav people. As a result, a new term made its entry. As early as 1848, the name Yugoslav appeared in the records of the Croatian Sabor as a substitute for the prohibited word Illyrian (Hondius, 1968, p. 59).

Map 4.4 Illyrian Provinces

Map prepared accordin to Magocsi, Paul R., *Historical Atlas of East Central Europe*

In the 1860s Austria suffered a military defeat from the new nation-states, Italy (Solferino, 1859) and Germany (Koniggratz, 1866). This setback weakened its internal position so much that demands for reform of its highly centralized political system could no longer be ignored. The Croatian Sabor called for an independent status for a Triune Kingdom (Austrians, Magyars, and Croats), on equal footing with Hungary. In response to the Croatian Sabor, however, the Austrians worked out an agreement with Hungary that again treated Croatians as a secondary political entity. The 'Ausgleich' (Compromise) in 1867 gave the Austro-Hungarian Monarchy a dual structure in which Hungary became completely autonomous, while the Croatians had to accommodate their status to the Hungarians. The Croatian question had been negotiated in 1868 by 'Nagodba' (Subcompromise) with Hungarians (Hondius, 1968; Curtis, 1992). According to Hondius (1968), it was considered that the 'Nagodba' was an act of union between two unequal partners, giving Croatians a provincial status short of statehood. This status of Croatia lasted until 1918, when Croatia renounced the 'Nagodba' and joined other South Slavs in a new state.

History and origin of Serbian national identity and statehood

First Serbian states

The first Serbian states emerged in the Balkans in the regions of Zeta (Duklja) and Raska. The rulers of Raska were first mentioned in the ninth century, but only upon the weakening of the Byzantine Empire at the end of the eleventh and beginning of the twelfth century did Serbian rulers see their chance to unify and create a powerful Serbian state. With Stefan Nemanja (1171-1196), a strong line of Serbian rulers commenced. Nemanja, born in Zeta, welded Zeta and Raska together (map 4.5).

Nemanja's dynasty succeeded in giving the Serbian State its own political and religious foundation. His son Stefan the First-Crowned (1198-1228) received from the Pope the crown and title of King. Nemanja's other son, Rastko, at an early age became a monk under the name of Sava and lived on Mount Athos, where with his father he founded the monastery of Hilandar. When he returned to Serbia, he obtained in 1219 from the exiled Byzantine Emperor in Nicaea permission to found a Slav-Serbian patriarchate. This was regarded as the most important event in the history of Serbian nationhood. Sava was canonized after his death.

Map 4.5 The Serbian state under Stefan Nemanja

Map prepared accoding to Magocsi, Paul R., *Historical Atlas of East Central Europe*

Serbian power reached its zenith under Stefan Uros IV, also known as Dusan the Great (1331-1355). In 1340 the Serbian state covered the territory between the Danube, Adriatic, Corinth, and Adrianople. In 1346, Dusan become Emperor of the Serbs, Greeks, and Bulgars (map 4.6).

Toward the rule of law in Serbia

Beginning in 1349, life in the Serbian state was regulated by law. In 1349 Dusan enacted the Code of Dusan (Dusanov Zakonik), which regulated family, criminal, and procedural law as well as the relationships between the estates. The Code contained elaborate rules on the position of artisans, cattle breeders (vlasi), clergy, landed gentry (vlastela), and hereditary nobles. An elaborate court officialdom demonstrated the might of the ruler with glittering titles. Dusan's court had a vast array of Byzantine-inspired dignitaries (such as despot, cesar, seastokrator, enohijar, sevast, etc.).

Dusan the Great died in the midst of preparations for an assault on Constantinople. With Dusan's death the rapid decline of the Serbian Empire began. His successor Uros (1355-1371) was not able to balance the power between the Serbian nobles. In meantime, the Turks were ready to invade the Balkans.

Battle of Kosovo and decline of Serbia

Disunited, the Serbs were not able to stop the Turks. Their last effort to stop the invaders was made at the Kosovo Polje. So strong were the memories of the Battle of Kosovo Polje that they became the most important historical event in the perception of the Serbian nationhood. On the feast day of St. Vitus (Vidovdan), 15 June 1389 (28 June in the Gregorian calendar), the Serbs, led by Prince Lazar and joined by the Bosnians, led by Stefan Tvrtko, were defeated by the army of Sultan Mourad I. Both Mourad and Lazar lost their lives in the battle. Losses were so significant on both sides that, even though militarily defeated at Kosovo, the Serbs succeeded in stopping the further incursion of the Turks. For some time, the conquered Slavic realms continued a semi-independent existence in the Turkish shadow. Two rival cousins, Vuk Brankovic and Stefan, minor son of Lazar, continued to rule and fight over what remained of Serbia (which in a treaty of 1443 was divided into Hungarian and Ottoman spheres).

Only after the Turks had recuperated from their losses at the Battle of Kosovo did Mohamed II liquidate the Byzantine Empire in 1453 and advance toward the remaining Serbian lands. In 1459, the fortress of Smederevo, the last stronghold of the Serbian Despotovina, was captured by the Turks. Bosnia became the next victim of the Turkish invasion; it was occupied in 1463 (map

Map 4.6 The Serbian state under Dusan the Great

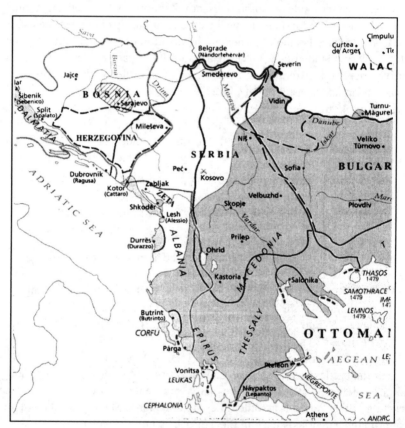

Map prepared accoding to Magocsi, Paul R., *Historical Atlas of East Central Europe*

4.7). Suleiman the Magnificent completed the invasion by capturing Belgrade in 1521.

The sixteenth, seventeenth, and eighteenth centuries were for Serbs the darkest period in their history. It was the period when they lost both their statehood and their basic political and human rights. Hondius (1968) explains the event in this way: 'The Turks drew a sharp boundary between the class of rulers and the lawless mass of subjects, the rayah. This boundary coincided with the distinction of nationality and religion. With the Slavic rayah, an internal levelling process took place. The native chiefs were dismissed by the Turks. Those Slavs who joined the Turkish ruling caste ipso facto became Turks. The landlords were usually absentees, living in towns' (p. 45). The author further describes a French traveller who visited Serbia in the seventeenth century and wrote that the villages where Serbs lived were far from the roads where the soldiers would pass. In the towns he visited he found only Moslems (Turks, Arabs, Persians) and foreigners (Greeks, Magyars, Jews).

Serbian national consciousness and patriarchate as a state

Oppressed and deprived of their own political institutions and political rights, the Serbs turned for solace to their language and their faith. Re-establishment of the Serbian Patriarchate in 1557 at Pec proved to be one of the most important historical events for the protection of Serbian tradition and identity. This autonomous institution took the role of the Serbian state within the Ottoman realm.

In 1690, however, as a result of further deterioration and abuse of human and religious rights of Serbs in the Ottoman Empire, the Serbian Patriarchate was forced to move to Austria. About 100,000 Serbs moved to Austria with Patriarch Arsenie Crnojevic. This was the most significant migration of Serbs in the Balkans in many centuries.

Serbs in the Hapsburg realm

In the times of medieval Serbia, Belgrade, a hill-fortress on the rivers Danube and Sava, marked the northern limit of Serbian territory. To the north lay the great Danube plain. Once the Turks had pushed into the plain and controlled all the territory up to Vienna, many Serbs followed them and settled the abandoned land. When the Sultan's forces withdrew, Serbian settlers stayed behind and became Hapsburg subjects. They were joined by other Serbs seeking refuge from Turkish oppression in 1690.

Though political and religious autonomy was promised to the Serbs in the Austro-Hungarian realm, it was never realized. The most they got was the

Map 4.7 Turkish occupation of Bosnia

Map prepared according to Magocsi, Paul R., *Historical Atlas of East Central Europe*

separate status of military frontier districts governed directly by authority in Vienna.

National awakening and statehood

The early nineteenth century was marked by the beginning of a strong Serbian awakening and reestablishment of Serbian statehood, followed by unification with other South Slavs at the beginning of the twentieth century.

Since the Serbs had little opportunity for cultural and political development within the Ottoman realm, the Serbian cultural activity took place in the diaspora. Vuk Karadzic (1787-1846), who is considered the father of Serbian literature, lived in Vienna, and the cultural society 'Matica Srpska' resided at Novi Sad, in South Hungary.

The First Serbian uprising of 1804 started as a local revolt against the misrule of the Sultan's men. In 1805, Serbian insurgents led by Djordje Petrovic, also known as Karadjordje (Black George, 1768-1817), captured the citadel of Belgrade and took the government into their own hands. Karadjordje's efforts to get some assistance from abroad in support of Serbian independence failed since most of Europe was occupied with Napoleon. As a result, Karadjordje was obliged to leave Serbia. Once ignited, however, the Serbian movement toward independence and statehood could not be stopped by Turks anymore. In 1815, Milos Obrenovic (1780-1860) led the Serbs in a second uprising. Partly by arms, partly by negotiation and use of Turkish weaknesses, Milos gained recognition of Serbian autonomy.

In 1830, Serbia become a vassal state subordinate to Turks under Milos Obrenovic. It became obvious that Milos' leadership style was not much different from that of the Turkish Pashas. His authoritarian approach met fierce resistance from the Serbs. In 1835, the Serbian Great National Assembly forced him to accept a Constitution. Events that followed in 1838 (a new constitution) led Milos to abdicate in 1839. The period in Serbian history (1838-1859) after the abdication of Milos was known as the Regime of the Defenders of the Constitution.

In 1869, a new constitution brought Serbia almost complete sovereignty. In 1875, Serbia declared war on the Turks, resulting in victory and international recognition of her independence. At the Peace Treaty of San Stefano, Russia declared Serbia independent, while at the Peace Conference in Berlin in 1878, Serbia was finally recognized as a sovereign and independent state. Four years later, Prince Milan Obrenovic assumed the title of King.

In 1888, Serbia again got a new constitution that recognized the concept of popular sovereignty, reflected in a powerful one-chamber Parliament. In 1889, King Milan Obrenovic was forced to retire and his son Alexander took the throne. His authoritarian leadership style led to his assassination. In 1903, a military junta killed him and called to the throne Peter I Karadjordjevic. While the two dynasties of Karadjordjevic and Obrenovic were fighting for the throne, political life flourished in Serbia. The chief opponents were the Progressive Party and the Radical Party. In 1903, the Radical Party split into a National Party (led by Nikola Pasic) and a Democratic Party. Halfway between Radicals and Progressives stood the Liberal Party of Jovan Ristic. There were also some other parties, but they didn't play a significant role in Serbian political life. During its independence Serbia developed a political culture significantly different from that of the Croats. While the Croats had been united as an ethnic minority group against the oppressive government dominated by Austrians and Hungarians, the Serbs were divided along political cleavages.

History and origin of Bosnian national identity and statehood

Bosnia is located between Serbia and Croatia. It has been populated since the sixth century by South Slav tribes of Serbs and Croats. Geographical location and historical development made Bosnia the crossroad of many cultures, religions, and civilizations. It was the place where the people had been molded by many invaders and rulers. Bosnia was the first victim of the great schism of Christiandom between Rome and Constatinople. As such, Bosnia fostered its own religion, called Bogumilism. During the tenth, eleventh, and twelfth centuries Bosnians were governed successively under different foreign rulers. When Hungarian crusaders ravaged their land in the thirteenth century, Bosnian nobles saw no solution to saving their privileges but to give up their own religion and convert to Catholicism (Hondius, 1968; Donia & Fine, 1994).

Bosnia reached its zenith in the fourteenth century under Ban Stefan Tvrtko (1353-1391), who became famous for bridging the differences between Catholics and Orthodox within the Bosnian realm. His acceptance of Catholicism kept the Pope and the Hungarians at bay, while his belonging to the Serbian Namanjic dynasty brought him the orthodox crown. In 1377, he was crowned King of Serbia and Bosnia at the Serbian orthodox monastery of Malesevo.

The invasion of Bosnia by the Turks in 1463 marked a new era in Bosnian history. Ottoman rule lasted for the next four centuries. The period between 1463 and 1878 brought significant social, cultural, and religious changes to Bosnia. The people were again molded by foreign rulers, this time by the introduction of Islam and Islamic culture (Hondius, 1968; Donia & Fine, 1994).

Under the Turks, the Bosnian nobles who once saved their privileges by converting to Catholicism again changed their religion. This time they turned

70

to Islam, a move that brought them the privileged status of the begs and agas. Over time they admitted not only the Turkish religion but also the life-style and culture of the Turks. One part of the Bosnian population followed their nobles; they converted to Islam and became the subject of complete islamization, while a still significant part of the population preserved their Catholic and Orthodox heritage, tradition, and culture. Those who converted became the Turks' surrogate rulers - a cause of major resentment by those being ruled.

In 1878, according to the agreement reached at the Berlin Congress (1878), Bosnia was occupied by Austria. This event marked the end of Ottoman rule in Bosnia and the beginning of a new era that ended with unification of the South Slavs into one state.

Awakening, statehood and movements towards unification

The early nineteenth century marked the beginning of South Slav awakening, while the early twentieth century marked the beginning of a new era - an era of South Slav unification. In the nineteenth century Croats moved toward the establishment of autonomy within the Austro-Hungarian Empire; Serbs moved toward reestablishment of their lost statehood; and Croats and Serbs in Bosnia struggled first with Turks and then with Austro-Hungarians for their freedom and independence. Events culminated in the unification of South Slavs in 1918.

Ideas about the unification of South Slavs had existed for many centuries, but historical and natural conditions were not in favor of such unification until 1918. Some of the ideas generated in the last two centuries require further elaboration.

Idea of unification (1)

In 1805, Karadjordje, the leader of the first uprising of Serbs under the Turks, in his communication to the Austrians, French, Russians, and other European powers, expressed the desire of the Serbs to unite with the Illyrian people. He was not able to draw the attention of the rest of Europe, and this idea was never realized.

Idea of unification (2)

Dositej Obradovic, who was one of the best-known Serbian authors (1742-1811), wrote repeatedly on the idea of unity for the South Slavs. He emphasized in his writings that the law and religion may differ among the South Slavs, but that birth and language did not. Despite the efforts of distinguished personalities, such as Dositej Obradovic, to keep the cultural consciousness of

71

South Slavs alive, the idea of a mutual political realm was not widely agreed upon.

Idea of unification (3)

During the Napoleonic era the Illyrian movement was introduced to the Balkans. Napoleon's victories in battle led to concessions from Austria. Provisions of the Treaties of Pressburg (1805) and Schonbrunn (1809) forced Austria to cede to France Dalmatia, Slovenia, and most of Croatia. Out of these territories Napoleon created the Illyrian Provinces, which he attached to his puppet Kingdom of Italy. France tried to provide a political structure and a national content to the Illyrian movement, and further they tried to develop national values for the Illyrians, such as an Illyrian language (Serbo-Croatian) and the like.

With the defeat of Napoleon and the return of the Illyrian provinces to Austria and later to Hungary, the Illyrian movement was suppressed and forced off the political agenda. Despite suppression, the Illyrian idea was taken up by the South Slavs within the Austro-Hungarian Empire in the 1830s, this time as an idea of their own. Continuous suppression and prohibition of the use of the terms that had reference to the Illyrian movement pushed the South Slavs to give up the Illyrian terminology, but not the Illyrian idea. Beginning in the 1850s, the Illyrian idea continued to exist with a new terminology consistent with South Slav unification - Yugoslavia.

Idea of unification(4)

A number of Croats brought new life to the Illyrian movement. Ljudevit Gaj (1809-1872) was one of the most prominent advocates among them, and Illyrism became a significant political movement under his leadership. His activity had been focused on Croatia, but his Illyrian ideas crossed the boundaries of Croatia, affecting the thinking of other South Slav intellectuals.

Idea of unification (5)

During the period of Serbian struggle for statehood and complete independence from the Ottoman Empire, Serbian Prince Mihailo Obrenovic, who reigned from 1860 to 1868, negotiated with the Bulgarians, Greeks, and Montenegrins as well as with Bishop Strosmajer, spokesman of the Hapsburg South Slavs, for unification of the Balkan people. His assassination in 1868 marked the end of this attempt.

The leader of the Croatian National Party, Josip Juraj Strosmajer (1815-1905), Bishop of Djakovo, set for his party two major goals. The first was to obtain Croatian independence and the second was to build Yugoslav unity. His generous endowment led to creation of the Yugoslav Academy of Arts and Science in 1867. His idea of Yugoslav unity led him to negotiation with Prince Mihailo of Serbia. Strosmajer believed that the different religious backgrounds were not obstacles for the unification of Catholic Croats and Orthodox Serbs.

It is also important to mention that during this same period in Croatia existed a strong opposition to unification with the Serbs. The Croatian Law Party (Stranka prava), founded by Ante Starcevic, advocated the reestablishment of Croatian statehood, but not unification with the Serbs. They considered religious differences between Catholic Croats and Orthodox Serbs an unbridgeable obstacle. After Starcevic's death in 1895, the right wing of the Law Party founded a new party, the Pure Law Party (Cista Stranka Prava), under the leadership of Josip Frank. The Pure Law Party followers had also been called Frankovci according to the name of their leader. They were anti-Serb extremists.

The First World War and unification of South Slavs

The First World War brought South Slavs together for the first time in history. Dissolution of the Austro-Hungarian Empire in the West and defeat of the Turks in the South created the conditions for South Slav unification. New international conditions, however, didn't bring unification alone; instead, it was the internal politics of the South Slavs and possible external threats in the future that forged the unity by both will and necessity.

There was more then one idea regarding how a unified South Slav state should look and what the character and internal structure of the state should be. The following ideas were pursued:

The South Slav state as an enlarged Serbia

Serbian Premier Pesic pursued the idea of an enlarged Serbia. He believed that it would be logical for other South Slavs to join Serbia, rather than to create a new entity. His assumptions were based on the fact that the Serbs had been victorious in the war for the liberation of South Slavs.

Union of the South Slavs into a new state

The opposition to an enlarged Serbia took a different point of view, advocating instead the union of the South Slavs into a new state. This approach meant that the State of Serbia would cease to exist. Differences between the two dissidents were resolved by the Serbian Assembly in 1915 when it declared that the aim of the war was the liberation and unification of the Serbo-Croat-Slovenian people. A similar idea was supported by the Yugoslav Committee (founded in Paris in 1915), which represented South Slav political exiles from the Hapsburg Empire. The immediate task of the Yugoslav Committee was to obtain support in France and England for South Slav liberation and unification.

South Slav State as a part of the Hapsburg realm

One group of South Slavs within the Hapsburg Empire, led by Antun Korosec, had a different agenda. The members wanted to preserve the Hapsburg realm, at the same time providing Croats, Serbs, and Slovenes with a new autonomous state within the Hapsburg Empire.

The Corfu Declaration

The Serbian Government, led by Pasic and the Yugoslav Committee, led by Ante Trumbic, met on Corfu for a conference in 1917. On 20 July 1917, the conference ended with a joint declaration on the creation of a single kingdom of South Slavs. The preamble of the declaration, written by representatives of the Serbs, Croats, and Slovenes, stated that the South Slavs are one people of the same blood, having a spoken and written language, consciousness of its unity, the continuity and integrity of the territory in which they live together, and a common vital interest of their national existence.

Article 1 stated that the State of Serbs, Croats, and Slovenes, also known under the name of South Slavs or Yugoslavs, would be a free, independent kingdom with a single territory and a single citizenship. It would be a constitutional, democratic, and parliamentary monarchy headed by the Karadjordjevic dynasty, which had given evidence that in ideas and feelings it did not differ from the people and that it placed the freedom and the will of the people above everything.

Article 2 specified that the state would be called the Kingdom of the Serbs, Croats, and Slovenes, and its head the King of the Serbs, Croats, and Slovenes.

Articles 5 and 7 formulated the legal equality of the 'triune nation', of its two alphabets and its religions. Article 14 of the Declaration provided that the organization of the future state was to be decided after the War by a sonstituent assembly.

With the Corfu Declaration the ideas of an enlarged Serbia and South Slav state within the Hapsburg realm were abandoned.

Preparation of the Hapsburg Slavs for unification

In 1918 the political representatives of the Hapsburg Slavs increased their activity toward dissolution of the Austro-Hungarian Empire. They followed the example of the Czechs by creating national committees. Activity culminated on 8 October 1918, when a National Council of Slovenes, Croats, and Serbs was proclaimed. The National Council declared itself the political representative of all Slovenes, Croats, and Serbs who lived in Croatia-Slavonia with Fiume, in Dalmatia, Bosnia and Herzegovina, Istria, Trieste, Carniola, Gorica, Styria, Carinthia, Backa, Banat, Baranja, Medjumurje, and the other parts of Southwest Hungary. Korosec, Slovene, Korosec was elected President of the Council. The Serb, Svetozar Pribicevic, and the Croat, Dr Ante Pavelic (a different person from the later Ustasa Pavelic), were elected Vice-Presidents. The National Council's only objective was the unification of all Slovenes, Croats, and Serbs and the establishment of an independent state of Slovenes, Croats, and Serbs.

In a series of events that followed establishment of the National Council, the Croatian Sabor dethroned the Hapsburg ruler and renounced the Nagodba as well as the union with Hungary. Sabor also officially recognized the National Council as Croatia's lawful government. Regional national councils in Dalmatia (Split), Bosnia (Sarajevo), and the Vojvodina (Novi Sad) also followed by declaring their adherence to the Council.

The National Council's objective was to be an equal partner with the Serbian Government in representing the Yugoslav case at the Paris Peace Conference. In order to achieve this equality, the National Council empowered the Yugoslav Committee to represent them abroad as the government of the South Slavs of the former Austro-Hungarian Monarchy.

The Act of union

At the end of November, the National Council sent their representatives to Belgrade to negotiate an immediate merger with Serbia. The National Council had been under pressure to achieve agreement with Serbia since the regional national councils, because of their own problems, were already threatening to join Serbia on their own. All members of the National Council had the same objective, namely, unification. Differences appered, however, when the specifics of implementation arose. The Dalmatian regional government wanted a more centralized state in order to protect itself from the Italians, while Stjepan Radic, leader of the Croatian Peasant Party, wanted a loose federation in which executive power would be held by three regents - the Prince Regent of Serbia, the Ban of Croatia, and the President of the Regional Government in Slovenia.

The deputation from the National Council arrived in Belgrade on 28 November 1918. They had Instructions (Naputak) prepared by the National Council for this occasion. Instructions had been negotiated and approved by most parties associated with the National Council; only the Croatian Peasant Party led by Stjepan Radic did not approve them. The Instructions emphasized that the final organization of the new state would be accepted with a two-thirds majority of votes cast in the Constituent Assembly. It was further emphasized that the Constituent Assembly should decide on the form of government and whether the new state should be a monarchy or a republic.

The act of unification was finally achieved on 1 December 1918 when a delegation of the National Council, headed by Dr Ante Pavelic, met with Prince Regent Alexander and members of the Serbian Government. Dr Pavelic read an address in which he stated that 'the South Slavs of the former Austro-Hungarian Monarchy . . . desire and are willing to unite with Serbia and Montenegro in a single State of Serbs, Croats, and Slovenes, which should embrace the whole uninterrupted ethnographic territory of the South Slavs.' He further stated:

> It is the resolution of the National Council that His Majesty King Peter, that is in his place as Regent Your Royal Highness, shall exercise the task of ruler over the entire territory of the now united State of Serbs, Croats and Slovenes, and that at the same time, a single parliamentary government shall be formed on the territory of the Yugoslav State as well as a national representative body, in agreement between the Government of Your Royal Highness and the representatives of all national parties in Serbia, and Montenegro (Hondius 1968, p. 90) (map 4.8).

In comparison with the Instructions, it appears that the National Council (or perhaps the Delegation at its own initiative) dropped the important question of the republican alternative.

In his address of reply, Regent Alexander proclaimed the Kingdom as a fact, saying:

> In accepting your communication, I am convinced that I am thereby fulfilling my duty as a ruler, for thereby I definitely concur with the work which the finest sons of our blood, of all three religions, all three tribes on both sides of the Danube, Sava and Drina already commenced during the reign of my forefathers Prince Alexander I and Prince Mihailo, which corresponds with the wishes and views of my people, so

Map 4.8 The First Yugoslavia

Map prepared according to Magocsi, Paul R., *Historical Atlas of East Central Europe*

now in the name of his Majesty King Peter I, I proclaim the union of Serbia with the lands of the independent State of Slovenes, Croats and Serbs into a single Kingdom of the Serbs, Croats and Slovenes (Hondius 1968, pp. 90-91).

International conditions

The end of World War I coincided with the beginning of a new world order. The United States President, Woodrow Wilson, played an important role in developing the principles upon which the new order should be constructed. These principles presented supportive international conditions for the formation of the first unified South Slav state.

Wilson believed that the old order based on the system of autocratic states and the lack of fit between nations and states were the major causes of war. He advocated that the new world order be based on particular kinds of states - democracies founded on the principle of nationality. He suggested that the peace would have to redraw the map of Europe so that nations and states coincided; and he considered the principle of self-determination as crucial for forging such a world order (Holsti, 1991, pp. 184-85).

Wilson exercised significant influence on the final peace settlement at the Paris Peace Conference. His concept of self-determination was used as a benchmark in the process of creating the new map of Europe even though his ideal type of nation was hard to find in reality. However a national boundary was drawn, some minority ethnic groups were always left within the new state. In the context of self-determination, this meant that recognition of the rights of one 'self' (the nation) entailed a denial of the rights of a competing 'self' (a minority ethnic group). Other questions in the implementation of the concept of self-determination also needed to be solved. One such question was related to the method of expression of the will of the 'self.' It was questioned whether plebiscites were the only legitimate method, or whether some other forms of representation could be used.

At the end of the First World War, all the historic units of the Austo-Hungarian Empire that were indisputably South Slav in the majority (Bosnia and Herzegovina, Dalmatia, and Croatia-Slavonia), along with the Kingdom of Montenegro, proclaimed their union with the Kingdom of Serbia, as presented earlier in this chapter.

South Slavs under the Austro-Hungarian Empire, short of statehood, used the right of self-determination to separate from Austro-Hungary and join a newly created state of South Slavs. In the process of creating the first South Slav state, the national identities of Croats, Slovenes, and Serbs in Austro-Hungary were recognized and used as the basis for self-determination and statehood.

Their process of statehood development was not completed, however, because the title of historic territory where they lived was not given to any of the smaller ethnonational units, but instead to the broader national unit of the South Slav state.

The process in the Kingdom of Serbia was significantly different. Serbs already enjoyed the benefits of independent statehood; therefore, before they could join the other South Slavs in a mutual state, they had to give up their statehood. As such, the Kingdom of the Serbs, Croats, and Slovenes was a product of Serbian and Montenegrin states and historic regions where the Croats, Slovenes, Serbs, and Moslems had lived under the Austro-Hungarian Empire. The self-determination of the Croats, Slovenes, Serbs, and Moslems from the Austro-Hungarian Empire was thus never completed since the territorial boundaries of their own states had not been determined.

This solution was driven by the assumption that the Serbs, Croats, Slovenes, and Moslems would develop a sense of one nation, which nation-state would be the state of South Slavs. In addition, the creation of the first South Slav state was a product of negotiation among the political leadership rather than of the will of the people expressed through a plebiscite. Creation of the new world order at that time, despite the rhetoric about the people's right to decide, was in reality based on elitist negotiation and bargaining. As was mentioned earlier in this study, a plebiscite was not used in any case of creation of the new European states. Serbs, Croats, and Slovenes were no exception.

If the objective of the new world order was to achieve an order where nations would coincide with states, this objective was compromised in the case of Yugoslavia. Despite the noble ideas of South Slavs to become one nation, the social, cultural, religious, and political realities were quite different. The South Slav nation-state remained the sum of different ethnonational identities rooted in long and different histories.

Conclusions

A nation-state is a political phenomenon that has appeared in the last two centuries. A nation-state is commonly defined as a polity of relatively homogeneous people who are governed by some of their own members. A nation is considered to be such a polity of more-or-less homogeneous people specific to time and place. There is no national population in the world, however, that shares complete homogeneity; there are only those who approximate an ideal type. The creation of the Kingdom of the Serbs, Croats, and Slovenes was based on an idea of the homogeneity of the South Slavs. The international community appeared to regard such a nation-state as the civic polity of South Slavs which would provide the nation of South Slavs with their own state, assuming that the supreme loyalty of Serbs, Croats, and other South Slavs was due to a nation-state of South Slavs. Such an assumption of supreme loyalty was built upon the ideas of unification developed in the prior two centuries among South Slav intellectuals and politicians driven by events in France and the popularity of the idea of the nation-state. Unfortunately it was not supported by any evidence of popular will. The history of the long-divided lives of Croats and Serbs was ignored despite the differing origins of their nationhood and statehood. Concerns about the future of a unified South Slav state by some politicians, such as the Croatian peasants' leader Radic, were not seriously considered by the domestic and international political establishment.

The Corfu Declaration of 1917 on the creation of a single kingdom of South Slavs underlined the affirmation that the South Slavs were one people: the same in blood, in spoken and written language, in consciousness of unity, and in the continuity and integrity of the territory in which they live together. In reality, though, the Declaration was, however, rather an effort to emphasize the ethnic and civic sources of cohesion of a future South Slav state. The cleavages that divided them, such as religion, culture, and political history, were not seriously considered as possible factors that could threaten the future existence of the unified state. Most importantly, there was no evidence to support the idea of the people's consciousness of their unity. The evidence suggested that the people were rather conscious of their Slovenian, Croatian, Serbian, or Moslem identity.

The historic Croatian struggle to gain independence was not completed. Croatia was compensated with a unified state that they had to share with Serbs and other South Slavs. Disintegration of the Austro-Hungarian Empire created an opportunity for the Croats, Serbs, and Moslems who lived in the former Empire (deprived of their rights) to have their own state, and to decide on their future. They still faced the problem of how to divide the territory among themselves in order to establish independent states. There were only historical regions where Croats, Serbs, and Moslems lived together within the larger realms of the Austro-Hungarian and earlier Ottoman Empire. These historical regions did not coincide with either Croatian or Bosnian medieval states. Moreover, the only administrative boundary between the Croats and Serbs that existed in the Austro-Hungarian Empire was that of a military frontier. Since every nation was envisioned to have the right to self-determination and its own state, the Croats and Serbs could create their own states along the territorial boundary of a military frontier. In the case of the historic region of Bosnia and Herzegovina, there were no such administrative lines at all. An intermingled population of Serbs, Croats, and Moslems was impossible to divide without population transfers. As such, they were destined for a mutual state. Such difficulties led the international community to effect a compromise. The concept of a unified state of South Slavs was supported over that of separate states of

South Slavs. It was expected that the nation-building process would create a national identity of South Slavs in a unified territory without previously having created independent states with a defined territory of ethnonational units.

In the next chapters it will be shown how these compromises of the domestic and the international political establishments greatly affected the political life of the Yugoslav state. Sources of national disintegration ignored at the creation became a major item on the agenda of the first and second Yugoslav states.

5 The first Yugoslav state

From the very beginning of the first Yugoslav state in 1918, the new state faced the difficult task of nation-building and ethnic conflict management. Although the same people, the South Slavs, differed significantly on the question of how the new state and nation should be organized and developed, most of the differences came as a result of cleavages deeply rooted in the history and origins of Serbian and Croatian ethnonational identity and statehood.

The political power of some politicians who disputed the legitimacy of the first South Slav unified state was underestimated in the process of unification. The political will of the people had not been tested on the questions of unification and the future form of the state. As a result of these competing forces, balancing the forces of national cohesion and dissolution became the major task of a new state. Once created, the South Slav state struggled throughout its history for survival.

In this chapter the effectiveness of the first Yugoslav state in regulating ethnic conflict between Croats, Serbs, and Moslems is analyzed, and the impact of Croat ethnic politics and mobilization on state stability is assessed. Domestic, perceptual, and international factors are used to explain particular events and time periods. The First Yugoslavia had the task of reconciling the ethnic differences of South Slavs and strengthening the unity of the newly created nation-state. Efforts were made by the King and other government officials to develop a national consciousness within the South Slavs and to create institutions that would provide a framework for mutual life. In these activities they were competing with ethnic nationalism of a separatist-minded Croatian peasants' leadership during the entire life of the First Yugoslavia. As such, the expectation of the domestic and international political establishments at the end of the First World War that the creation of a unified South Slav state would contribute to nation-building of a South Slav nation was tested.

Ethnic conflict management at the beginning and the first constitution

One of the major opponents of unification was the Croatian peasant leader Stjepan Radic. His opposition was expressed before unification when he had demanded a 'neutral peasant republic of Croatia.' Shortly after the unification he became the leading spokesman for Croatia and Croatia's right to self-determination. In his efforts to create an independent Croatian state, he repeatedly asked President Wilson and other representatives of foreign states for help (Dragnic, 1983, p. 18).

Coercion (hegemonic control)

The immediate response of the inexperienced, provisional government to Radic's separatist activities was to put him in jail. He was imprisoned the first time in March 1919, when he spent nearly a year in prison. Upon his release he resumed his separatist activities. As a result, he was almost immediately rearrested in March 1920. In August 1920, Radic was sentenced to two and a half years in prison. The upcoming elections for the Constituent Assembly seemed to soften coercive government policy, however, in dealing with the separatist movement. Radic was released on the day of the elections for the Constituent Assembly, 28 November 1920.

Election for the Constituent Assembly

The election for the Constituent Assembly was the first real test of popular support for the new state. The total number of seats was fixed at 419. There was one member for every 30,000 people, with one additional delegate for a surplus of 17,000 or more for each of 55 districts. Popular response to the election was overwhelming, 65 percent of the eligible voters cast ballots.

Twenty-two political parties or groups participated in that election. Five parties with national platforms won a large majority of the seats. The Democrats had candidates in every one of the 55 districts and the Radicals had candidates in 47 of them.

The combined popular vote of the five national parties was as follows:

	Votes	Delegate Elected
Democrats	319,448	92
Radicals	284,575	91
Communists	198,736	58
Land-toilers	151,603	39
Social Democrats	46,792	10
Total	1,001,154	290

According to these figures from Beard and Radin (1929), it was clear that a large majority of the voters in the new kingdom were not primarily concerned with maintaining sectional independence. The authors go on to show that these five parties differed mainly among themselves with respect to the form of the new government, but none of them was bent on the development of autonomist political rights at all costs or federalism at any price. There were, however, three important parties with primarily sectional interests. These were:

	Votes	Delegates Elected
Croatian Peasant Party (Radic)	230,590	50
Slovenian Populist (Korosec)	111,274	27
Yugoslav Moslems	110,895	24
Total	452,759	101

Beard and Radin further stressed that among them the Croatian Peasant Party was the most extreme in its separatist claims.

The regional distribution of seats by party provide a clearer picture of the distribution of political power within the unified state. Democratic, Radical, and Communist parties were most successful in obtaining seats from diversified regions: (1) The Democratic Party was most successful in Serbia (32 seats), Kosovo and Macedonia (24), and Croatia (19); (2) The Radical Party was most successful in Serbia (41), Vojvodina (21), and Bosnia and Herzegovina (11); and (3) The Communist Party was most successful in Kosovo and Macedonia (18), Serbia (14), and Croatia (7). The Agrarian Party was most successful in Serbia (14), and the Slovene People's Party suceeded in Slovenia (14). The Croatian Republican Peasant Party elected delegates only in Croatia and the Yugoslav Moslem Organization only in Bosnia-Herzegovina. Only 342 out of 419 elected representatives presented their credentials. Of those who did not present their credentials the largest group was the 50-member Croatian Peasant Party (Dragnic, 1983, p. 21).

Croatian separatist policy

The Croatian Peasant Party led by Radic captured nearly all of the Croatian delegates in the election for the Constituent Assembly. The parties supportive of unification that had represented Croatia in the provisional parliament were decisively defeated. Dragnic (1983) points out that the results of the election were interpreted by Radic as a mandate to create a separate Croatian state.

Immediately after the elections for the Constituent Assembly, about 80,000 members of the Croatian Republican Peasant Party met in Zagreb on 8 December 1920. They proclaimed the Neutral Peasant Republic of Croatia and took an oath to the Croatian homeland and Croatian Republic. The 50 elected representatives who had not presented their credentials to the Constituent Assembly joined the separatist declaration.

Development of Constituent Assembly decision-making principles

The Constituent Assembly convened on 12 December 1920, at which time it adopted rules concerning the process of decision making. One of the most important rules to be adopted was on voting for the Constitution when it was submitted to the full assembly. It was a controversial item since different proposals had been submitted for consideration. One group advocated an absolute majority of the total membership; another group favored two-thirds of total membership; and yet another group supported a majority of those present. Finally it was decided that the constitution would be adopted only if an absolute majority of the total membership voted for it. In practice this meant that the future form of the state of the pluralist multiethnic society of the Kingdom of the Serbs, Croats, and Slovenes could be decided without the agreement of any one of the major constituent ethnic groups - Croats, Serbs, or Slovenes.

Constituent Assembly on the form of the state

During the debate over the Constitution, several constitutional drafts were presented and considered. In the absence of Radic's Croatian Peasant Party representatives, the issue of unification and the principle of parliamentary monarchy were not questioned, although the constitutional proposals did vary from a unitary to a federalist form of government. The basically unitary versions also included a considerable amount of local self-government for the historical regions (varying from six to twelve). The Agrarian Party submitted a draft that embodied a form of corporativism, with a parliament consisting of representatives from different fields of endeavor. But when it came time to decide the leaders of the two dominant parties, Pribicevic (Democrat) and Pasic (Radical), agreed that the state should be organized on a unitary basis. This latter position prevailed.

Major constitutional propositions

Regardless of the outcome, it is interesting to examine the proposals submitted for consideration and their differing ideas on the form of the state. Some proposals favored centralization while others favored a more or less decentralized federal system.

Stojan Protic's draft (Radical Party) represented a compromise between the two extremes of centralized vs. decentralized state. Protic's proposal advocated building the national government based mainly on the English parliamentary model. It proposed a creation of nine provinces corresponding roughly to the historical sections into which the Kingdom was divided, with a significant level of local autonomy.

The Croatian plan advocated creation of six district provinces: (1) Serbia and Macedonia; (2) Croatia, Slavonia, Dalmatia, Istria and Medjumurje; (3) Montenegro; (4) Bosnia and Herzegovina; (5) Vojvodina; and (6) Slovenia. Each of these provinces was to have an independent government, and the constitution of the Kingdom could never be changed except with the unanimous consent of the parliaments of the provinces. Resembling the U.S. Constitution, the Croatian plan stipulated that the central government would have only those powers expressly delegated, that all other powers should be reserved for the local parliaments.

The third plan was drafted by autonomists from Slovenia, who advocated federalism in politics and state socialism in economics. The draft recommended that the country be divided into six provinces similar to the Croatian plan but slightly different in regard to the boundaries. Its objective was to form three Catholic and three Orthodox states.

A fourth plan, drafted by Dr Smodlaka but not formally presented, proposed a scheme that divided the country into 12 provinces, dismembering even Croatia and Serbia.

The proposal that got the most attention was the one drafted by the Pasic cabinet. It recommended a unitary system of government with a democratically elected unicameral parliament, the ministers being responsible to it and to the king. It was the concept of a constitutional parliamentary monarchy more concerned with the balancing of power between the king and the parliament than between the different ethnic groups. It was a constitution that assumed the Kingdom of the Serbs, Croats, and Slovenes was a homogeneous nation rather than a heterogeneous multiethnic nation.

The Pasic cabinet draft resembled the Serbian Constitution of 1903. It was supported by Democrats and Radicals whose political platforms advocated a more cohesive centralist state. Beard and Radin (1929) argued that Pasic was a centralist by conviction who feared the Croatian and Slovenian spirit, which had acted as a dissolving force in the Austro-Hungarian Empire. According to them, Pasic believed that any federal system would lead to the disintegration of the Kingdom of the Serbs, Croats, and Slovenes.

None of the proposals were able to get a majority of votes based exclusively on the support of their drafters, nor were any of the political parties or ethnic groups able to dominate the agenda. There was no political party or ethnic group with an absolute majority in the Kingdom of the Serbs, Croats, and Slovenes. As such, it was important to produce a compromise and build alliances between some political parties as well as between different ethnic groups in order to pass the constitution.

The majority of the drafters supported the Pasic cabinet draft, since the Democrats and Radicals stood behind it. By themselves, however, Democrats and Radicals did not have enough votes to pass the constitution (210 votes were needed to pass a constitution). They then entered into negotiations with a number of small parties. Pasic managed to get the support of the Yugoslav Moslems and some other small parties.

In the vote on the final Pasic cabinet draft on 28 June 1921, 258 representatives voted - 223 for, 35 against, while others abstained, including the representatives of the Croatian Peasant Party. The 223 votes in favor were distributed as follows: 184 Serbs, 18 Moslems, 11 Slovenes, and 10 Croats. The constitution was proclaimed on the Serbian national holiday Vidovdan (28 June), and thereafter came to be known as the Vidovdan Constitution.

It is important to mention that the majority support for the Constitution drafted by the Pasic cabinet was obtained through political negotiations among the Serbs, Croats, Slovenes, and Moslems affiliated with different political parties. Democrats and Radicals who had been largely under Serbian leadership were not able to dominate the procedure alone. A compromise was reached with the Yugoslav Moslems, who represented mainly the landlords of Bosnia and Herzegovina, and other small parties that brought the unitary state into being. The major group not supporting the Constitution, the Croatian Peasant Party and its leader Radic, had elected not to participate in the political debate and decision-making of the Constitutional assembly.

Territorial organization of the state

Under the 1921 Constitution, the Kingdom was divided into 33 provinces. In general, this division was made with reference to topography, population, former administrative units, economic interests, and old sectional areas such as Croatia, Slovenia, and Bosnia. As a rule, the boundaries of the provinces did not cut across sectional borders, that is, they conformed to the lines of the historic districts composing the kingdom. Among themselves, the provinces differed materially in size and population. The largest had 798,000 inhabitants; the smallest 109,000.

At the head of each province stood a high administrative officer, the Great Zupan, or Prefect, appointed by the Minister of the Interior and responsible to the central government in Belgrade. As expressed by law, the Great Zupan was to be an old and experienced civilian officer. According to the terms of the statute, he had to hold a degree in civil law and have had 15 years of government service. Legal training and administrative competence were the prime qualifications, in theory at least and to a considerable extent in practice. In ordinary practice, the Great Zupan was a civilian officer representing the central government in his province.

Croatian ethnic policy of separatism and accommodation

Despite the new constitution, Radic continued to work for Croatian independence, which, if successful, would have led to the dismemberment of the Kingdom. He intensified his activity both abroad and at home, making extraordinary efforts to gain the support of the international community. In particular, he solicited help from the United States and France. In August 1922, he submitted a memorandum to the League of Nations asking the League to recognize the Neutral Peasant Republic of Croatia. In March 1923, however, Radic changed his policy within the Kingdom. His party took part in the national election and won 70 seats. Using this base, he was more inclined to collaborate with other opposition leaders in order to defeat the Pasic government and provide support for Croatian independence, possibly in confederation with Serbia.

Radic's domestic platform included (1) recognition of the Karadjordjevic dynasty as a symbol of the Yugoslav union; (2) a Croatian constitution that would provide for legislative power in the territory of Croatia (Croatia-Slavonia-Dalmatia); (3) Croatian membership in the League of Nations; (4) foreign affairs, trade, and defense to be administered in common, but the organization and use of the national army in Croatia to be decided by the Croatian parliament; (5) autonomy for Slovenia, Montenegro, Bosnia-Herzegovina, Macedonia, and Vojvodina - similar to that in Croatia; and (6) all legislative authority in Croatia to belong to the Croatian parliament with executive power to be in the hands of a Ban (governor) selected by the Croatian parliament to whom alone he would be responsible (Dragnic 1983, pp. 32-33).

Government policy of coercion and accommodation

The government of the Kingdom did not have an adequate response to the Croatian separatist policy. Radic's separatist activities abroad and the impatience of Pasic's government led to Radic's arrest in 1925. Despite Radic's imprisonment Pasic continued to work on a political solution with him and his followers. A policy of accommodation was replacing the policy of coercion and hostility. Radic moderated his position against the Constitution, proclaiming that he did not seek revision of the Constitution so much as eventual change based on people's needs after a trial period. Pasic also declared that the Constitution was neither permanent nor perfect. These statements allowed them to make an agreement in July 1925. This agreement opened the way for a Pasic-Radic Cabinet, stipulating that one of the tasks of the new cabinet was to implement the Constitution in the whole territory of the Kingdom of the Serbs, Croats, and Slovenes. Immediately after the agreement was reached, all charges against Stjepan Radic were dropped and he were released from prison.

Radic's change of direction, whether a new tactic or a real change of attitude, brought new light to the Kingdom. This new opportunity for a mutual life of Serbs, Croats, and other South Slavs was also recognized by the government and the King, leding to an accommodative government policy towards Radic's party rather than to a policy of coercion and suppression.

The period of reconciliation following the Pasic-Radic agreement did not last long. Differences between the two leaders soon became obstacles. Stjepan Radic, who joined the cabinet as Minister of Education, found himself under pressure from his former supporters who accused him of working with ministers he had criticized in the past. As early as February 1926, Radic suggested the need for a revision of the Constitution, asserting that he had not given up his earlier program. In April 1926, the inability of the cabinet to reach a compromise led to Radic's resignation, the fall of the cabinet, and the end of Pasic's long career in political office.

Dragnic's (1983) findings in his research on the work of the Pasic-Radic cabinet in 1925-1926 are useful in understanding the political behavior of Croats and Serbs in this mutual state. Dragnic was able to identify two distinct categories of political terminology. In the speeches of Croatian politicians there was a constant reference to Croatian rights, the Croatian nation, and the Croatian state. In contrast, Serbian politicians used such terms as cabinet, party, elections, coalition, and opposition. Scarcely ever were Serbdom, Serbian national thought, or Serbian interests mentioned. These differences in political terminology most likely came about as a result of differences in Croatian and Serbian histories and in the origins of their nationhood and statehood. It appears that Croats simply transplanted their oppositional political behavior from the Austro-Hungarian Monarchy, which they had perceived as suppressor of their individual rights and statehood to the new united Kingdom. Serbs appeared to base their political behavior on the assumption that Serbs and Croats were the same people, so the major concerns for them were related to key political concepts of government.

After the fall of the Pasic-Radic coalition. Stjepan Radic was able to remain as Minister of Education in the new Radical-Radic cabinet formed by Radical Nikola T. Uzunovic. However, the Radical-Radic coalition ended in 1927, marking the end of the politics of compromise between the Radical Party and the Croatian Peasant Party. In a search for new alliances, Radic approached the independent democrats who represented Serbs living together with Croats in the Austro-Hungarian Empire. On 10 November 1927, Radic and Pribicevic, the leader of the Democratic Party, concluded an agreement establishing the Peasant-Independent Democratic coalition. The intended character of the coalition was spelled out in Radic's assertion: 'We Croats and Serbs are one people, especially we Croats and Serbs who lived together . . . and we as one people (those outside Serbia) should have one free state' (Dragnic, 1983, p. 47).

His remarks on Croats and Serbs as one people opened a new page in his strategy for realizing his separatist platform, this time by dividing Serbs and developing a coalition with those Serbs who were not able to dominate overall Serbian politics in the Parliament.

The obstructive behavior of the Peasant-Democratic coalition led to parliamentary paralysis and to resignation of the cabinet in February 1928. For the first time, Radic got a chance to form a cabinet on his own. When King Alexander offered him this opportunity, he accepted the offer, but his efforts to form a new cabinet were not successful. He was not able to come to an agreement with the Radicals, who refused to enter his cabinet.

Increasing polarization and hostility marked political life in that period. Radic and Pribicevic, as leaders of the coalition shifted their activity from parliament to a broader public audience. Together they raised the issue of constitutional revision. In a speech in Dubrovnik in May 1928, Radic insisted that the country be divided into four or five large regions, each with considerable powers of self-government. He again threatened to pull his representatives out of the Parliament in Belgrade. Externally, the Peasant-Democratic coalition appealed for support in Western Europe on the constitutional revision issue, but got no encouragement (Dragnic, 1983, p. 50).

In June of 1928 it became almost impossible to keep Parliament in order. Bitter conflicts between the Radicals and the coalition were the order of the day The mutual attacks and insults led to carnage in the Parliament on June 20. In one heated debate, Punisa Racic, a radical Serb from Montenegro, pulled out a revolver and killed or wounded a number of coalition representatives. Stjepan Radic was among the wounded. After a brief recovery, he died two months later in Zagreb. Racic was later tried, convicted, and sentenced to 20 years' imprisonment. The remaining Cabinet resigned on 4 July 1928. (Dragnic, 1983).

The end of parliamentary democracy

Immediately after the carnage in the Parliament, the Peasant-Democratic coalition moved their headquarters from Belgrade to Zagreb, announcing that they would no longer participate in the work of the national Parliament. They demanded the dissolution of the Parliament and a revision of the Constitution.

The inability of the political parties to compromise and the extreme positions of the Peasant-Democratic coalition pushed King Alexander to consider suspension of the Constitution and establishment of a nonparliamentary regime. According to Dragnic (1983), Alexander was concerned with the fact that in ten years the South Slav people had not been able to achieve a common tradition. It was obvious that the ten-year period of mutual life was not long enough for the processes of nation-building to succeed, particularly in a society burdened with ethnic cleavages rooted deeply in centuries of separate life.

In one of his last efforts to overcome the crisis, King Alexander asked Macek (Radic's successor) and Pribicevic if they were willing to work toward an agreement with other political parties. They rejected the offer, asking instead for a prior change in the political system that would alter the unitary character of the Kingdom. In addition, Macek asked for reestablishment of the old historical regions with their own parliaments and executive power. He envisioned the following autonomous units: Slovenia, Croatia, Bosnia, Vojvodina, Serbia, Montenegro, and Macedonia.

King Alexander, unable to bring all political parties to the negotiating table, concluded that there was no parliamentary solution that would guarantee the preservation of a full state and national unity. Consequently, he announced on 6 January 1929 that he was temporarily assuming personal rule. He declared it was his sacred duty to guard 'national unity and the integrity of the state,' which 'must be the highest law for me and for everyone.' The time has come, he added, 'when there cannot, and must not any longer, be an intermediary between the people and the king.' The parliamentary system, he declared, threatened to destroy the unity of the state and was an impediment to all productive work. It was necessary to 'seek new methods and blaze new roads' (Dragnic, 1983, p. 76).

Announcement of the personal rule of King Alexander did not come as a surprise at home or abroad. Dissolution of parliament and abolition of the Constitution were consistent with Macek's demands and preconditions for the political reorganization of the state. Alexander's assumption of personal power was generally approved abroad. The King received the strongest support from leading governmental circles in France and Czechoslovakia, while Britain remained somewhat reserved. Most of the criticism came from Italy, Hungary, and Bulgaria, whose leaders were known to be hostile to a united South Slav state. The criticism from these states nevertheless, served to bolster Alexander's support in the states that supported a united South Slav state.

Introduction of the name of Yugoslavia as a means of nation-building

In the fall of 1929, King Alexander had taken additional steps to secure consolidation and unity of the state. He changed the name of the country to the Kingdom of Yugoslavia, giving a new meaning to the state of the South Slavs. The Kingdom of Yugoslavia was expected to be more than the simple sum of the South Slavs. It was the beginning of a long-term process of creating a Yugoslav nation. At the same time, the country's 33 administrative districts were reduced to 9. The new administrative regions were called Banovinas, following the Croatian term for a region ruled by Ban. The boundaries of the Banovinas were to conform to natural boundaries of waterways rather than traditional historical lines (map 5.1). It was most likely the intention of the King to overcome the old ethnic cleavages developed throughout history and to start Yugoslav nation-building from the top by giving a new name to the Kingdom and from the bottom by creating cross-cutting administrative regions.

Guided democracy

In September 1931, Alexander's personal rule was brought to an end, and he replaced personal rule with an Octroyed Constitution. The new political system was later known as 'guided democracy.'

The Octroyed Constitution proclaimed Yugoslavia a hereditary constitutional monarchy, with the king as champion of national unity and integrity of the state. It provided for a representative system, but added an upper house (Senate), half of whose members were to be chosen in electoral colleges in the Banovinas, and the other half appointed by the king (46 Senators were elected, but the king never appointed his full quota). The new Constitution retained the unitary system, but with a degree of decentralization. Banovinas were recognized as self-governing units with elected councils that would choose their executive organs. The Constitution was soon followed by an electoral law permitting the formation of political parties. The formation of political parties that opposed national unity and the integrity of the state was not permitted.

Map 5.1 The boundaries of the Banovinas

Continuing policy of separatism and government coercion

The new Constitution did not bring a framework for political settlement in the Yugoslav Kingdom. Student demonstrations in 1931-32, led initially by Belgrade University students, demanded the return of freedom to the people and a federal system. For many Yugoslavs the new order was simply a continuation of personal rule.

In his assertions from this period Macek again repeated his claims for a more independent Croatia within the Yugoslav Kingdom. This time he signaled that he wanted (1) to know which areas would make up Croatia, (2) a precise indication of the powers of Croatian self-ruling institutions, and (3) local armed forces to be established to guarantee (1) and (2). From his statement to a French newsman in June 1932, it is possible to better understand his attitude toward Kingdom of Yugoslavia. He said: 'Yugoslavia is like a man with an incurable disease, who certainly will soon die. The death will liberate Croatia' (Dragnic, 1983, p. 93). This statement suggests that Macek did not look for a solution within the existing state, rather it was a restatement of retrieval of separatist policies in opposition to the Yugoslav state.

In 1932, the Peasant-Democratic coalition was still alive. On 7 November 1932, in Zagreb, the coalition adopted a resolution that proclaimed (a) the people were the sole source of political power; (b) the peasantry should be the foundation of organized public life; (c) Serbian hegemony had been imposed on non-Serb areas and strengthened by the 'absolutist' regime of 6 January 1929; (d) in order to get rid of Serbian hegemony it was necessary to return to the situation of 1918, that is, prior to unification; and (e) a new organization of the state, based on agreement among all of the peoples of the state, was needed. As a result of this resolution, Macek was arrested in December 1932.

The Slovene People's Party followed with a resolution similar to that from Zagreb. In January 1933, the Slovenian Peoples Party leader, Anton Korosec, was arrested. Following the Korosec arrest, the Slovenian People's Party came out with a new resolution, which made clear that the demands did not jeopardize the integrity of the Yugoslav state. In January 1933 the Yugoslav Moslem Organization also associated itself with the Peasant-Democratic coalition. The Moslem's resolution, however, was milder and its leader, Mehmed Spaho, was not arrested but only fined.

The demand of Croatian, Slovene, and Moslem leadership and political parties for more autonomy and separation suggests that there was at least a perception of Serbian domination.

Croat extremism and assassination of King Alexander

The inability of Croats to impose their solution on the nation led to the formation in Croatia of extremist groups; these had already been particularly active abroad. Their frustration culminated in the assassination of King Alexander in October 1934 during his visit to France. The assassination was engineered by the Croatian extremist organization Ustashi, operating out of Italy and Hungary.

Alexander's reputed last words, 'Safeguard Yugoslavia,' tended to endow his memory with a heroic political mystique and dedication to the Yugoslav nation. For those South Slavs who wanted Yugoslavia to survive, he entered eternity as a hero of Yugoslav unity rather than a Serbian hegemon. But, his death was not the only event that brought him a reputation as a sincere Yugoslav. Much earlier he had named his second son Tomislav after Croatia's first king. He gave his third son the Slovenian name Andrej. His assumption that all South Slavs were the same people did not help him in the process of nation-building. Specifically, he was unable to recognize the significance of historical differences in the origins of the Croatian and Serbian ideas of nationhood and statehood. The different political practices that these two ethnic groups brought to the new state proved to be a major obstacle in organizing political life within that unitary state. Nine hundred years of subjugation appeared to have made the Croats resistant to any form of mutual life despite the early indications of some Croatian intellectuals. Croatian desperation led to extremism and later to assassination of the Yugoslav King. The King's belief in the idea of a united Yugoslavia cost him his life. Serb involvement in, and support of, a unitary state was perceived, especially by the Croats, as a form of domination that also fueled the resistance to further 'subjugation.'

At the time of his assassination, Alexander's eldest son, Peter, was only 11 years old. Therefore, the royal powers were assumed by a regency of three men. The first regent was Prince Paul Karadjordjevic, Alexander's first cousin. A Radical, Stojadinovic, was named as Prime Minister in 1935. As a Radical stalwart and an opponent of dictatorship, his appointment was viewed as the beginning of the end of authoritarian regimes. Expectations that Stojadinovic would be able to reconcile with the Croats and to rejuvenate the Radical Party proved to be unwarranted. He was not successful, and as a result Prince Paul asked him to resign, which he did on 3 February 1939. Dragisa Cvetkovic, who had been Minister of Social Policy in the Stojadinovic Cabinet, was named the new Prime Minister.

Rise of Fascism in Germany; Ethnic claims and accommodation in Yugoslavia

Stojadinovic believed that his failure to find a solution to the Croatian question was not the primary reason for his removal. Rather, he saw the rise of Hitler in Germany as the reason for the new international situation and his removal. In January 1939, the Croatian representatives, led by Macek, adopted a resolution urging the Great Powers to intervene in Yugoslavia to assure the Croats 'liberty of choice and destiny' (Dragnic, 1983, p. 111).

The dismemberment of Czechoslovakia tends to support Stojadinovic's belief. It appears likely that the destruction of that nation made Prince Paul more concerned for the future of Yugoslavia. Macek took advantage of the situation by asking Prince Paul for several concessions. Prince Paul, concerned with the events in Europe, was ready to reach an agreement that would satisfy Croatian demands without changing the existing Constitution. Macek kept raising his demands. His emissary, Ivan Subasic, in his talks with Prince Paul, concentrated his efforts on the territorial recognition of a big Croatia. At first, Subasic indicated that the Croats wanted to bring together the Savska and Primorska Banovinas in a Croatian territorial unit. At the second visit, he added Dubrovnik, and at the third the Vrbaska Banovina (northern Bosnia). Finally, on the fourth visit, he asked for other territories - a part of Srem, Brcko and environs, Bijeljina, Travnik, Fojnica, and Hercegovina (essentially all of historical Croatia, Dalmatia, and Hercegovina, plus all of northwestern Bosnia and a few territories in northern Bosnia).

Use of the foreign threat as a form of ethnic policy

Macek's claims for more and more territory were accompanied by use of the foreign threat. In an interview with a correspondent of the New York Times on 1 August 1939, Macek declared that if Croatia did not gain autonomy, it would secede from Yugoslavia, even though this would lead to war and Croatia might thereby become a German protectorate. Macek's aggressive policy accompanied with the threat of fascism in Europe and his intended alliance with fascist forces, brought him concessions.

Macek and Cvetkovic reached an agreement on 20 August 1939, which was approved by Prince Paul on August 26, 1939. The Croatian Banovina (Big Croatia) was created by the agreement. It included the pre-World War I territory of Croatia and most of Slavonia, together with Dalmatia and parts of Bosnia-Herzegovina. Approximately one-fourth of the Banovina's total population of 4.5 million were Serbs. The Croatian Banovina created its own parliament (Hrvatski Sabor) and its own governor (ban).

Collapse of the First Yugoslavia

The Cvetkovic-Macek agreement was signed on the eve of the Second World War, which broke out in September 1939. Poland was quickly defeated, and Belgium, Holland, and France fell in the spring of 1940. The rapid fall of France and the inability of Great Britain to deter Hitler's Germany and Mussolini's Italy from further expansion was a severe blow for Yugoslavian foreign policy, traditionally oriented toward the West. In addition, Yugoslavs were divided; Croat and Slovene leaders were in favor of aligning with the Germans and signing the Tripartite Pact (German, Italy, Japan), while the Serbs (including Cvetkovic) were leaning toward the West. Since Cvetkovic and Prince Paul were aware that a war with Germany would be national suicide, they tried to stay neutral but were not able to achieve this status. Under German and domestic pressure Cvetkovic signed the Tripartite Pact on 25 March 1941 (Dragnic, 1983, p. 132).

A military coup and popular protests in Belgrade followed the signing of the Tripartite Pact. On the night of March 26-27, a military coup overthrew the Cvetkovic-Macek cabinet. The coup leaders ousted Prince Paul by declaring young King Peter of age. The new cabinet was headed by General Dusan Simovic, a Serbian leader. Events in Belgrade angered Hitler so much that he ordered a massive attack on Yugoslavia, with Belgrade as a particular target. On 6 April 1941, German airplanes bombed Belgrade, inflicting heavy casualties and material damage. Yugoslavia, not ready for war and internally divided, collapsed within two weeks. Defeat led to dismemberment of the country. The Croats were the first to use this event as an opportunity. Under the leadership of the Croat extremist, Ante Pavelic, and sponsorship of Germany and Italy, the Independent Fascist State of Croatia was created, with boundaries that extended beyond the boundaries of the Croatian Banovina, occupying the new territories of historic Bosnia (map 5.2). In addition, parts of Yugoslavia were ceded to Italy, Hungary, and Bulgaria, while the remainder was divided into Italian and German occupation zones. The young King Peter, with most of the cabinet members, fled abroad.

Conclusions

The First Yugoslavia resembled a big laboratory for social, political, and administrative engineering. The objective of the experiment was to test whether a constitutional monarchy and a unitary state could provide South Slavs with an institutional framework that would peacefully reconcile and accommodate their historic differences.

97

Map 5.2 Independent Fascist State of Croatia

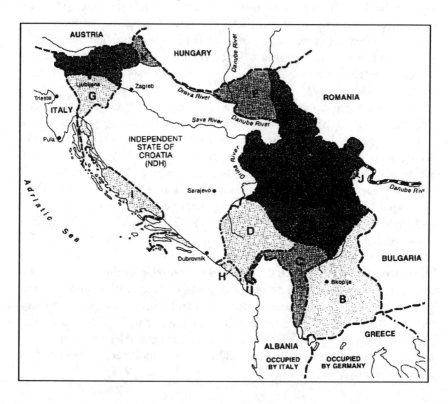

The Serbs and Croats who were joined in the unified state did not have enough knowledge and sensitivity to each others' histories of nationhood and statehood to make it work. The Serbs, led by the concepts of majoritarian democracy where a simple majority would rule the country with a multiparty system organized on the bases of political preferences rather then ethnic differences, did not understand that their ethnic majority status would be perceived as a threat to other groups in a majoritarian system of government. Thus they were able to get only marginal support for the constitution and political institutions that resembled their most recent statehood experience. On the other hand, the Croats, led by the experience of an oppressed ethnic minority without recent independent statehood, were not willing to integrate into a system mostly inherited from the Serbian state. Almost exclusively, they supported one party that represented Croats as an ethnic nation within the unified state and continued to behave as they had behaved when they were part of the Austro-Hungarian Empire. They perceived the Kingdom of the Serbs, Croats, and Slovenes as they perceived the Austro-Hungarian Empire, as an entity that was suppressing their nationhood and statehood.

The Serbs, who gave up their statehood in order to accept a broader statehood based on a South Slav nation-state, appear not to have understood these differences. Trapped in their own paradigm of political and administrative institutions, they refused to recognize the Croats' needs for a separate national identity and state. The idea of a federal system with a built-in protection of minority rights was not a part of Yugoslav thinking during this period.

The assumption that mutual life would bring them together was based on Illyrian and other movements for the unification of South Slavs. The popular will of the Croats, however, was not tested at the creation of the unified state. As it became clear in all the later elections during the entire life of the First Yugoslavia, the Croats demonstrated the weakness of the 'Illyrian' assumption. The Croatian Peasant Party consistently won popular support for its agenda of separation. In addition, the resistance of the Croatian people to a mutual state grew with the imprisonment of their leadership and their inability to enforce their own agenda for at least partial separation.

In response to Croatian demands, the King and the government used coercive and accommodative methods of ethnic conflict management. Coercive methods such as imprisonment, authoritarian rule, and prohibition of political parties to pursue nationalistic agendas did not end the problem. The change of name from Kingdom of the Serbs, Croats, and Slovenes to the Kingdom of Yugoslavia in the process of nation-building, and the efforts of King Alexander to present himself as the King of Yugoslavia also failed because of the lack of readiness of the South Slavs to accept a new Yugoslav identity.

Accommodation of Croatian demands was also tried through changes in the Constitution and the building of government coalitions, but claims of the Croats remained unfulfilled. The Croats wanted their own state and a government to govern it. The major problem of having their own state, however, was the problem of territorial boundaries. They wanted to divide a single territory of South Slavs into independent regions - administrative units that could later be used as the basis for the ethnonations to exercise rights of self-determination and secession.

The Croats gradually achieved their goal on the eve of the Second World War. They used the threat of Fascism, and later open support of Fascist Germany and Italy, to create a Croatian Fascist state that extended far beyond the boundaries populated by Croats, occupying regions of the former Austro-Hungarian Empire where the Serbs lived, and Bosnia and Herzegovina where the Serbs and Moslems shared the land with Croats. They created a greater Croatia on the ruins of the first unified South Slav state. And more than this, despite the fact that Croats and Serbs had never directly fought each other, the Croats' extreme policy of ethnic conflict management, as will be elaborated in the next chapter, led to genocide and expulsion of the Serbs and others who had shared the land and life with them for centuries. Mutual life with Serbs in the First Yugoslavia and dissatisfaction of Croats with that state's political institutions and coercive policies could not and should not justify their extreme policy under World War II Fascism.

6 Creation of the Second Yugoslavia and Tito's era

In this chapter the international, domestic, and perceptual factors that led to the creation and political cohesion of the Second Yugoslavia are analyzed. The sources of national cohesion and disintegration are identified and analyzed throughout Tito's era. In particular, this analysis covers the role of the international community during the Second World War and on the eve of the Cold War, the role of the liberation and communist movements, the role of Tito, the role of the Communist Party and its ideology of socialist self-management. Government efficiency in ethnic conflict management is analyzed through the elaboration of constitutional development.

Dismemberment of the First Yugoslavia

The Second World War was disastrous for the First Yugoslavia. All of the neighboring states joined the Axis powers; as a reward, most of them got a piece of Yugoslavia. Germany, Italy, and their allies divided Yugoslavia into ten parts, with Croatia benefiting the most. While Belgrade lay in ruins, recuperating from Hitler's bombing, Zagreb was preparing to welcome combined Fascist forces. On 10 April 1941, when German troops entered Zagreb, the new Fascist Croatian state was proclaimed.

The most extreme Croatian politician, Ustasa Ante Pavelic, took power on 15 May 1941. Immediately he announced his strategy of ethnic conflict management and nation-building in Fascist Croatian state. That policy resulted in up to one million Serbs and others being put to death. Pavelic's regime used the formula 'One-third of Serbs will be killed, one-third will be driven out of Croatia, and one-third will be converted to Catholicism.' Estimates of the number of Serbs killed vary from 300,000 to more than a million. A generally accepted figure is 500,000 to 700,000. The same policy was followed toward the Jews and the Gypsies; the number of Jews killed was about 50,000, and the number of Gypsies around 20,000 (Dragnic, 1992, pp. 102-03). According to Serbian Orthodox Church sources in 1941 and 1942, about 800,000 orthodox Serbs were killed, about 300,000 had been driven out, and about 250,000 were converted by force to Catholicism in Croatia (Stranjakovic, 1991). Kostich's (1981) collection of documents on the Holocaust in the Independent State of Croatia, based on German, Italian, and other sources, support the above-mentioned figures.

The impact of these events on the image of Croatian nationalism, and especially on relations between Serbs and Croats who lived through the war, remains an important factor in Yugoslav politics and society to this day (Burg, 1983). The Ustase massacres and other incidents of racial warfare in Yugoslavia - such as between Serbs and Moslems - left a traumatic vacuum in the memory of those who lived to remember them (Hondius, 1968).

Remnants of the First Yugoslavia

The Cabinet and King Peter in exile continued to represent Yugoslavia internationally. Domestically, upon the capitulation and dismemberment of Yugoslavia, remnants of the Yugoslav army under the command of Colonel Draza Mihailovic withdrew to the Serbian Ravna Gora mountains refusing to surrender to the Germans. The objective of the Chetnik movement led by Mihajlovic was to keep the Serbian countryside under control, defeat the Germans, and, with help from the Allies, bring back the Royal Government (Hondius, 1968; Burg, 1983).

Movement for the Second Yugoslavia

In the middle of 1941 there was no one left on the domestic front to fight for the Yugoslav idea. This gap was soon filled by the Communists, led by Josip Broz Tito. They saw their chance while fighting Fascism to bring a new social, political, economic, and administrative order to Yugoslavia. Their goals had been dictated mostly by the Russian-dominated Comintern and by the idea of unification of the entire world's proletariat. With 12,000 party members at the outbreak of the War, the Yugoslavian Communist Party was able to successfully organize a nationwide uprising (Hondius, 1968). The Communists declared war on the foreign occupiers, while attributing the fall of Yugoslavia to the old regime. They developed the concept of guerilla warfare, which brought them a lot of success. The Partisans' struggle for liberation and independence, which included all South Slavs, became known as the 'People's

Liberation War'. The liberation of Yugoslavia from all occupiers was the major objective of the resistance and uprising. The revolutionary context of the war was not emphasized at the beginning of the war, but with success on the battlefield and their rising popularity among the population, the partisan movement led by the Communists shifted its activity more and more toward creation of a new Yugoslav state that was much different from the pre-war one.

Tito's personnel policy in a process of building the Second Yugoslavia

Tito, Croato-Slovenian by origin, chose people of differing ethnic backgrounds for his closest associates. They included: Mosa Pijade (a Serbian Jew), Edvard Kardelj (Slovenian), Aleksandar Rankovic (Serb), Milovan Djilas (Montenegrin), Rade Koncar (Croat), and Ivo-Lola Ribar (Croat from Serbia). His cadre policy supported his purpose to bring all South Slavs into one state again.

Proclamation of the Second Yugoslavia

Already in 1942, partisans had organized a governing structure. The possibility for partisans to create a real government occurred only after Italy surrendered to the Allies in September 1943. The new Yugoslav state was proclaimed on 29 November 1943 in Jajce, the one-time capital of Bosnian kings. The AVNOJ (Antifascist Council of People's Liberation of Yugoslavia), as representative body of the Partisan's Liberation Movement from all regions of pre-war Yugoslavia, reconstructed Yugoslavia as a federal state. The decisions of their first meeting were laid down in three resolutions. The first resolution referred to the governing structure. AVNOJ transformed itself into 'the supreme representative of the sovereignty of the people and of the State of Yugoslavia as a whole' (Article 1) and, as such, into 'the supreme legislative and executive representative body of Yugoslavia for the duration of the People's Liberation War' (Article 2). A Presidium was appointed (Article 3), consisting of 67 members with Dr. Ivan Ribar, a Croat from Serbia, as Chairman. This body in turn appointed a National Committee for the Liberation of Yugoslavia, which had 'all the marks of a people's government' (Article 7). The Committee consisted of 13 members and was headed by Tito.

The second resolution of AVNOJ denied the Royal Government in London any right to act as the legal government and representative of the Yugoslav people (Article 1). The Resolution further forbade King Peter II to return to the country (Article 2). The third resolution stated as follows:

The peoples of Yugoslavia never recognized and will never recognize the dismemberment of Yugoslavia by the fascist imperialists and have shown in the joint armed struggle their firm will to remain united and further to unite in Yugoslavia. (Article 1)

In order to realize the principle of the sovereignty of the peoples of Yugoslavia and to make Yugoslavia a true fatherland of all its peoples and never again the domain of any clique whatsoever, Yugoslavia is developing and will develop according to the federative principle, which will guarantee full legal equality to the Serbs, Croats, Slovenes, Macedonians and Montenegrins, respectively to the peoples of Serbia, Croatia, Slovenia, Macedonia, Montenegro and Bosnia and Herzegovina. (Article 2)

To national minorities in Yugoslavia all national rights are guaranteed. (Article 3)

It is important to mention that, as indicated by Hondius (1968), during the discussion of Article 2, the Bosnian delegate, Sulejman Filipovic, was pressing the drafters to include 'Moslems' in this article as a national group. His proposal was not admitted. A compromise was made by adding the line 'respectively the peoples of . . . Bosnia and Herzegovina' (pp. 129-30).

Although the resolutions stipulated the major characteristics of the new state, many questions were left to be answered after the war. One such question was whether Yugoslavia would be a republic or a monarchy. This was partially a tactical decision because the Allies were still ambiguous about whom to support: the Provisional Partisan Government or the Royal Government in exile.

The Yalta Conference and Yugoslavia

In 1945, with the Second World War approaching its end, the Yugoslav question became more salient in Allied discussions on the concepts of a new Europe. This time the problem of self-determination and unification did not dominate the agenda, rather, the major concerns were the regime type and the sphere of interest. The Cold War was emerging on the ruins of the Second World War, and the Yugoslav question was regarded as a part of the overall two-power struggle that would dominate the world for the next 45 years.

In October 1944, Churchill and Stalin reached an agreement in Moscow over the future of Yugoslavia and the Balkans. It was agreed that Yugoslavia would constitute a shared sphere of influence (McFarlane, 1988). As elaborated by

Churchill (1954), there was also a secret agreement between Stalin and Churchill that Yugoslavia would be divided into a 50 percent British and a 50 percent Russian sphere of interest while the war continued. Since this division reflected only two opposing positions regarding the regime type (western or communist) of the future Yugoslavia, at the Yalta Conference, held 4-11 February 1945, Churchill, Stalin, and Roosevelt decided to push for a long-term solution for Yugoslavia. They recommended that the leaders (Tito and Subasic) of the partisan and Royal Governments should jointly decide on the future of the Yugoslav political system and state formation (Trifunovska, 1994).

In August 1945, as was recommended at Yalta, a provisional Yugoslav government was formed out of partisan and royal representatives. The major objective of the provisional government was to prepare a constituent assembly. As was the case with the First Yugoslavia, the political system and state formation of the Second Yugoslavia was to be decided by a constituent assembly. Preparation for a new constituent assembly and elections was dominated by Communists. On election day there were only two choices: to support or not to support candidates of the People's Front (communists and their supporters). The People's Front gained 6,725,045 votes (90.48%), while 707,422 votes (9.52%) opposed their candidates (Hondius, 1968).

These results made it easy for the Constituent Assembly to bring a new Yugoslavia into being. On 29 November 1945, the Constituent Assembly unanimously proclaimed the establishment of the Federal People's Republic of Yugoslavia and the abolition of the monarchy. On the 1 December, Tito was appointed head of the Government. Finally, the Constitution draft prepared by Tito's closest associates was unanimously adopted by the Constituent Assembly on 30 January 1946 and proclaimed the next day.

The Constitution and the national question

As early as in 22 May 1945, in his speech to the city of Zagreb, Tito referred to the future federal character of the Yugoslav state:

> Many do not yet understand what is the meaning of federative Yugoslavia. It does not mean the drawing of a border line between this or that federative unit. . . No! Those border lines, as I see them, must be something like the white veins in a marble staircase. The lines between the federated states in a federal Yugoslavia are not lines of separation, but of union. This is community house, one whole, but inside, each must be master of himself and develop culturally and economically in a new federative Yugoslavia. (In Hondius, 1968, p. 180)

Tito's solution to the national question was based on Lenin's and Stalin's concept of self-determination. Tito argued:

> The national question with us has been solved and to be precise, solved very well, to the general satisfaction of all our nationalities. It has been solved in the way Lenin and Stalin have taught us. (Tito, 1948, p. 6)

Edvard Kardelj, one of the Tito's closest associates, in a speech broadcast by Radio Belgrade on 5 December 1945, addressed the main characteristics of the proposed Constitution. Concerning the national question, he argued that the nationality problem was liquidated, saying:

> The third important change in Yugoslavia is the new relationship between the peoples of Yugoslavia. The old system of hegemonistic greater-Serb cliques upheld by reactionary anti-national Croat, Slovene and other influences has been done away with. The Federative People's Republic of Yugoslavia has grown out of the voluntary unification of our peoples according to the principles of self-determination and equality of rights. Our peoples have signed their act of unification with their blood and have put the principles of self-determination and equality of rights into practice by building up the federal units and the united federative state community. In this way they have created all the conditions necessary for the liquidation of the nationality problem which constantly shook and undermined the old Yugoslavia. (Constitution, 1947, pp. 26-27)

The more or less same words used by Tito and Kardelj in their reference to the nationality problem in Yugoslavia were to be used for the next four decades. It was the beginning of the time when the national question could be ignored based on the Lenin and Stalin use of the concept of self-determination. With the strong Communist Party apparatus, which functioned on the principle of democratic centralism, the doctrine of self-determination was not applicable in reality. It was used more as part of the ideological game, having in mind that the separatist forces (largely Croat) who collaborated with Fascists were already militarily defeated.

From the very beginning, Communist Party leadership, as we can see from the Kardelj speech, portrayed the King and the Serbs as hegemons who had dominated the first Yugoslavia. The same position was clearly stated by Tito in his speech delivered at the Fifth Congress of the Communist Party of Yugoslavia. In accusing the monarchy of unitarism and national oppression, he said:

The Pan-Serbian hegemonists led by the king hoped to tone down the national struggle by bribing the leaders of various parties like Korosec (Slovene People's Party), Spaho (Bosnian Moslem party), etc., and with their help the regime got a majority in parliament and in the government against those Croats, Slovenes and others who were struggling against national oppression. (Political Report, 1948, p. 21)

Hondius (1968) also emphasized that the Programme of the Yugoslav Communists did not spare the Serbs from critical comment on the negative role in Yugoslav history of the 'Greater Serbian bourgeoisie' and of 'Greater Serbian hegemony' (p. 149). This position appears to be inherited from the Croats and their perception of Serbian domination.

The 1946 Constitution

The new Yugoslav Constitution was very much a copy of the Soviet Constitution of 5 December 1936 - the so-called Stalin Constitution. Edvard Kardelj commented on this by praising the Soviet Constitution: 'For us the model was the Soviet Constitution, since the Soviet federation is the most positive example of the solution of relations between peoples in the history of Mankind' (Krbek, in Hondius 1968, p. 137).

This remark by Kardelj revealed his own and Tito's early position, as well as the major concerns of the new political elite. It was imperative for the creators of the new social, political and economic order in Yugoslavia to find a solution for the nationalities question. Since the Soviet Union was the only socialist country available to use as a model, it was logical for them to use Stalin's Constitution as the basis for the new Yugoslav Constitution.

It should be noted that Stalin divided nationalities into two or more republics and also moved large numbers of people into these republics. The result has been that any former Soviet Republic attempting to secede from the larger political system must immediately confront one or more dissident minorities - a perfect formula for civil war. We are seeing the unfolding of these policies and the resulting civil wars today, not only in Yugoslavia but also in the former Soviet Union.

In Article 1 of the Constitution, the national question was immediately addressed as follows: 'The Federal People's Republic of Yugoslavia is a federal people's State, republican in form, a community of peoples equal in rights who, on the basis of their right of self-determination, including the right of separation, have expressed their will to live together in a federative State.' This article contained the message that the new Yugoslavia was a community of peoples who according to the Lenin and Stalin doctrine had used their right of self-determination by determining to live together. Given the fact of massive losses due to the War and the dominance of the Communist Party, this 'right' and the 'decision' was at best problematic.

The new Constitution assumed the existence of the five component peoples as defined by Jajce in 1943. Hondius (1968) observed that the Yugoslav federation indicated the peoples, not the Republics, as its basic components. This distinction was very important in recognizing Yugoslavia as a sum of people (nations) rather than a sum of nation-states.

However, when it came to federal units, Yugoslavia was divided into six republics, as regulated by Article 2: 'The Federal People's Republic of Yugoslavia is composed of the People's Republic of Serbia, the People's Republic of Croatia, the People's Republic of Slovenia, the People's Republic of Bosnia and Herzegovina, the People's Republic of Macedonia and the People's Republic of Montenegro.'

The People's Republic of Serbia is further divided by creation of two autonomous provinces. In Article 2 the Constitution stated: 'The People's Republic of Serbia includes the Autonomous Province of the Vojvodina and the Autonomous Kosovo-Metohija Region' (Constitution, 1947).

The new composition of Yugoslavia came as a result of the distribution of power in the top Communist Party leadership. Boundaries of internal division were drawn behind closed doors by Tito and his closest associates (map 6.1), (Djilas, 1991, p. 170). It should be understood that the new Yugoslavia was not created by integration of independent states with defined territories and internationally recognized boundaries. It was rather a partitioning of the Yugoslav state recognized by Yalta and the international community, based on the political power of members of the Communist leadership. It also reflected the intention of the political leadership to fight perceived Serbian hegemonism by partitioning Serbia.

In his study of this constitution Hondius (1968) argued that the Yugoslav Constitution and constitutional theory accepted the five component peoples and their six countries as given data. Further, that there was a conspicuous absence of any theory as to exactly why these nationalities found their political expression in various units of the Yugoslav federal state. Hondius continues:

> Technically speaking the establishment of the Yugoslav federal State has been rather unusual because it did not consist of the creation of closer union between hitherto independent or looser related States, but in the redivision of a State which was previously unitary. None of the six People's Republics mentioned in Article 2 existed in that form before, or independently from the Federation. The question arises whether a previous and separate existence of the component parts is a prerequisite for the existence of a federation. (p. 140)

Map 6.1 The Second Yugoslavia

The problems emphasized by Hondius should be considered as most important for the future of the Yugoslav nation and state. That is to say, in short, that the idea of one nation in proclamation was replaced by the idea of the sum of ethnonations in formal political institutions from the very beginning of the Second Yugoslavia.

The People's Assembly

The People's Assembly set up by the 1946 Constitution was a bicameral body composed of one all-Yugoslav chamber, the Federal Council, consisting of one representative for every 50,000 inhabitants, and another chamber representing the various People's Republics, called the Council of Nationalities. This Council was composed of 30 representatives for each People's Republic, 20 for the Autonomous Province of Vojvodina, and 15 for the Autonomous Region of Kosmet. The chief federal organs were defined as the People's Assembly, the Presidium, and the Government. It has been pointed out that the People's Assembly was envisaged as the supreme organ of unrestrained people's power. However, the real power was concentrated in the Presidium and the Government, whose officers were elected by the People's Assembly.

The most prominent function of the Presidium was the collective headship of the state. Its role was to accommodate the political aspirations of Tito's associates with diverse ethnic backgrounds. According to the Constitution, it was to be elected by the Assembly at a joint meeting of both houses, and was composed of a president, six vice-presidents, a secretary, and not more than 30 members. The idea was to keep political leadership from different regions in the center rather than to send them to their own regions - the Republics and Autonomous Provinces. This also allowed Tito to keep an eye on anyone who might challenge his leadership or the unity of the state.

Although the new Yugoslav state had a federal character according to the formal Constitution, the real power was concentrated in the center and executed through the administration copied from the Russian system of public administration. Vertical lines of command had priority over horizontal coordination and integration. One of the major replicas of the Soviet system in Yugoslavia was the set-up of the Federal-Republican Ministries. Although appointed by the Republics, the Federal-Republican Ministries at the Republic level were agents of the Federation. With extensive nationalization of industry, trade, and banking, the national economy was further brought under central management of the state. Only small crafts and a part of the agricultural sector were left in private hands. The Yugoslav state was highly centralized in the first couple of years after the Second World War. As Hondius (1968) summarizes it, the Yugoslav state was federal on paper, but highly centralized in practice.

110

Conflict with Stalin and decentralization

In 1948, after a series of disputes between Tito and Stalin concerning the development of Yugoslavia, the Cominform (an international organization for coordination between the Communist Parties) decided to expel Yugoslavia from the Communist movement. This decision was made on 28 June 1948, at a special meeting convoked in Bucharest by the Cominform. The Yugoslav Communist Party successfully resisted Stalin's pressure, and at its Fifth and Sixth Congresses (1948 and 1952 respectively), independently defined the direction for further development of the political, social, and economic system of Yugoslavia.

The experience with Stalin and the Cominform led the Yugoslav politicians and scholars to the conclusion that a highly centralized state with a planned economy was one of the major obstacles to future socialist development of Yugoslavia. As a result, from 1950 forward Yugoslavia again became a field for political, economic, and social engineering. A new set of reforms was introduced on the basis of democratic socialism. The first step was to reduce the size and scope of the federal administration, which counted 47,310 officials. As a result of reform in 1956, the federal administration was reduced to only 10,328 officials (Hondius, 1968, p. 191).

The major step toward a new socialist system, however, was the introduction of worker self-management. On 2 July 1950, the People's Assembly of the Federal People's Republic of Yugoslavia (FNRJ) transferred by a new law the entire management of economic enterprises and associations from state organs to the Workers' Councils of these enterprises. These Councils were elected by the workers' collectives. That law was the first of a series of successive institutional innovations in the postwar period (Schrenk, Ardalan & Tataway, 1979).

McFarlane (1988) recognizes that an important by-product of the introduction of workers' self-management was administrative decentralization. For example, the six Republics were given greater economic and political autonomy. Also, the decentralization of the economy initiated by the law significantly changed the position and attitude of local authorities. The People's Committees, which served as the organs of local government, recognized the significance of local industries in the generation of fiscal income for local communities. On 1 April 1952, the Federal Parliament adopted a General Act on People's Committees, reflecting the new position of the People's Committees.

The Communist Party was also a subject of reform. At the Sixth Congress in 1952 it changed its name to the League of Communists thereby reflecting a change in the role the Communist Party played in society. The new role was expected to be more leading than ruling. Power was expected to devolve toward the 'basis,' toward factories and communes. According to this idea, genuinely free discussions should take place there, and freely elected delegates should be sent to higher political bodies and assemblies. Through the workers' control of the economy and the citizens' direct democratic control over political bodies, self-management was meant to curb the power of the bureaucracy and the centralist state. Moreover, these processes were expected to move society toward the withering away of the state and the establishment of a classless and stateless Communist society (Djilas, 1991).

As presented, development of the Yugoslav self-management system in the next four decades was successful in withering away of the Yugoslav unified state. The major by-product, however, was development of extreme ethno-national policies of local and regional leaders, leading subsequently to violence, civil war, and dismemberment.

The 1953 Constitutional Law

The significant changes introduced by reforms of the political, economic, and social systems made the 1946 Constitution obsolete. As result, on 13 January 1953, the Yugoslav Assembly accepted a new act, entitled the Constitutional Law, to replace the old Constitution. The meaning of the Constitution was diluted and applied to a collection of laws (Constitution, 1960).

The Constitutional Law introduced a new division of work between the state and organized society based on the idea that the process of the withering away of the state should commence. This process was introduced with the 1950-52 decentralization and was systematized by the Constitutional Law under the heading of Workers' Self-government and local self-government. Management of the economic and social institutions was transferred from a restricted group of career officials to tens of thousands of workers and citizens. Also, control over the application of the system was handed over primarily to the organs of local government.

The new federal community

The same period brought a new approach to federalism. The political leadership stressed that the federation should no longer be regarded as the sum of the nationalities and their Republics, but as a new kind of socialist community, that is, a community of working people. In the words of Kardelj, the Yugoslav Federation had become 'above all a bearer of the social functions of a unified socialist community of the Yugoslav working people' (in Hondius, 1968, p. 194).

The changes in federal institutions followed the announcement of a new federal concept. The bicameral character of the new People's Assembly (federal parliament) was preserved, but the two former chambers, the Federal Council and the Council of Nationalities, were subject to change. The Council of Nationalities was abolished and a Council of Producers, elected by the producers in different branches of the economy, was created to reflect the argument that the new federation was rather a community of producers than a community of nationalities. The Federal Council retained its name but was changed in structure, part of its delegates being elected directly on the ratio of one delegate to every 60,000 inhabitants. The other part of the Council was composed of indirectly elected representatives of the Republics and autonomous units. The Republican Council of each People's Republic designated ten delegates, six were designated by the Provincial Council of the Vojvodina and four by the Regional Council of Kosovo-Metohija. The new Federal Council reflected in unicameral form the bicameral structure of the former People's Assembly of the FNRJ. The Council of Nationalities continued to exist, hidden behind the name of the Federal Council. Even the operations of the Federal Council were divided. Delegates who had been appointed by the People's Republics and autonomous units were obliged to isolate themselves from the others in a special session when the important constitutional questions were on the Agenda of the Federal Council. The objective was not to prevent delegates from participating in these issues but to force them to protect the interests of the Republics and autonomous units at first and then to look at the broader federal interests.

The Constitutional Law made two major changes in the executive system. The Presidium and Government were abolished and replaced by a President of the Republic and a Federal Executive Council. Tito was elected as the first President; his chief official function was to preside over the Federal Executive Council.

Toward a new constitution

The changes in the 1950s in political thinking and the introduction of democratic socialism followed by Constitutional Law created the conditions for a new constitution. The politicians felt the need to go from the experimental stage of a socialist democracy to full implementation of socialist self-management, a concept that had become the basic principle in public affairs. Ever since 1953, as the by-product of economic decentralization, Yugoslavia's six Republics had been allowed a greater degree of autonomy; consequently, new national rivalries and factions had been growing, thus making the debate more difficult.

The national question

In the process of preparing for the new constitution, the multiethnic character of Yugoslavia was emphasized, while the idea of one Yugoslav nation was not promoted beyond the concept of a community of ethnic groups.

In support of this new direction, on 20 September 1962, in a speech at the Federal Assembly, Kardelj declared: 'Our Federation is not a frame for making some new Yugoslav nation, or a frame from the kind of national integration which various advocates of hegemonism or denationalizing terror have been daydreaming of' (In Hondius 1968, p. 242).

Tito, in his speech to the same meeting emphasized commonality in socialist social relations as a major factor of unity by saying:

> When we speak about integration, we do not think of the integration of nationalities, of their assimilation or of the negation of the existence of different nationalities in our country. This is a matter which we settled long ago. There are several nationalities in this country and they all have their distinct histories and present-day life, and they are all developing independently their culture and internal life on the basis of their positive achievements in the past. . . . But there must be something that is common to us all. (p. 243)

The 1963 Constitution

The 1963 Constitution changed the name of the federation from Federative People's Republic of Yugoslavia to Socialist Federative Republic of Yugoslavia. The Introductory Part, Section I, outlined federalism in its relation to Yugoslav society as a whole. It said:

> The peoples of Yugoslavia, on the basis of the right of every people to self-determination, including the right to secession, on the basis of their common struggle and their will freely declared in the People's Liberation War and Socialist revolution, and in accordance with their historical aspirations, aware that the further consolidation of their brotherhood and unity is to their common interest, have united in a federal republic of free and equal peoples and nationalities and have founded a socialist federal community of the working people, the Socialist Federative Republic of Yugoslavia, in which, in the interests

114

of each people and of all of them together, they are achieving and developing.

Part One, Article 1, was more specific: 'The Socialist Federative Republic of Yugoslavia is a federal State of voluntarily united and equal peoples and a socialist democratic community based on the power of the working people and on self-government'.

It is also important to mention that the new constitutional formula recognized for the first time Moslems as a constituent people. The point is clearly stated in the Constitution of Bosnia and Herzegovina (Section I) when it refers to constituent peoples: 'Serbs, Moslems and Croats, allied in their past by a common life.' The addition of Moslems to the list of main peoples of Yugoslavia was an important amendment to the original list, as contained in the Second AVNOJ Resolution of 1943, and lent a recognition of their separate ethnic identity.

Self-determination, sovereignty, and secession

The emphasis on Yugoslav peoples rather than on a Yugoslav nation led to a reappraisal of the questions of self-determination, sovereignty, and secession. Implicitly, in Yugoslav theory and practice since 1946, it was considered that the Yugoslav peoples, by uniting into a federation in 1943, had made use of their right of self-determination and that the right to secession was thereby consumed (Hondius, 1968, p. 250).

With the new theoretical thinking, reaffirmation of the rights of the peoples to self-determination and secession under a new constitution came as a logical step in the process of decentralization begun in the early 1950s. It is important to note, by the way, that the rights of the peoples are recognized, rather than the rights of the Republics. This was clearly stated in Section I of the new Constitution quoted above.

The Federal Assembly

The new Constitution preserved the Federal Council and abolished the Council of Producers. Instead, it instituted four new chambers, representing the 'working people in the working communities' (Article 165): the Economic Chamber, the Chamber of Education and Culture, the Chamber of Social Welfare and Health, and the Organizational-Political Chamber.

The Constitution did away almost entirely with the system of direct election of deputies. All delegates now represented either the Municipalities or the Republics and Autonomous Provinces. The Federal Chamber was composed of 120 deputies elected by the assemblies of the Municipalities, plus 70 delegates elected by the Republican assemblies from among their membership (ten each) and by the Assemblies of the Autonomous Provinces (five each). Under the 1953 Constitutional Law, there was a link between the federal deputies and local government in the sense that the deputies of the Federal Council automatically held a seat in the People's Committee of their voting district. The 1963 Constitution reversed matters: the Municipalities had the right to send delegates to the Federal Chamber.

Tito and the new Constitution

It was felt that the Constitution should do justice to Tito's exceptional position and exempt him from the vagaries of Yugoslav politics. By virtue of a special provision in Article 220, it was determined that the rule of rotation would not be applied to the office of the President of the Republic as long as Tito was in office.

The Nations come of age

During the 1950s it was declared by Tito that the nationality question in Yugoslavia had been satisfactorily solved, but, as events later proved, a mere declaration does not make it so. By the middle 1960s tensions and conflicts among the nationalities began to reappear. The new domestic environment allowed the first reemerging nationalism, particularly in Croatia. The conflict between the center and the periphery ended with a purge of the Croatian nationalistic leadership. This was followed by the constitutional changes that ended in 1974 with a new Constitution.

The Eighth Congress of LCY and the new national policy

The 1963 Constitution dispersed decision-making power over a large number of self-governing units. Although each of them was autonomous in its own sphere, their freedom of action was limited by mutual dependencies. Only in the framework of a common general policy were their individual policies practicable.

The League of Communists was fortified by Section VI of the Constitution as the sole legitimate political party, but the new polycentrism of Yugoslav public life had its effect even on the League. The central position which the League continued to occupy was not in the first place a manifestation of power of the League itself, but the result of a growing need for a central forum in which the fundamental issues of public policy could be brought together and discussed.

After the enactment of the 1963 Constitution, three sets of problems dominated political discussion: the full implementation of self-government and self-management, general economic problems, and the relations between the nations.

In his report to the Congress (the Eighth Congress of the League of Yugoslav Communists convened in Belgrade from 7-15 December 1964), Tito held the middle road between those in favor of and those opposed to the super-nation when he said:

> There are persons, and even Communists, who think that nationalities in our socialist society have outlived themselves and should wither away. They confuse the unity of nations with the liquidation of nations and with the establishment of some kind of artificial, that is one single, Yugoslav nation, which is tantamount to assimilation and bureaucratic centralization, to unitarism and hegemonism. Yugoslav socialist integration is a new type of social community in which all nationalities find common interests. (In Hondius, 1968, p. 315)

The final resolution of the Eighth Congress rejected the idea of a Yugoslav uniform nation as being a 'harmful suggestion,' but it also warned against 'nationalism' and 'chauvinism.'

Nationalism in Croatia

The Declaration

While the revision of the Constitution of 1963, generated by a new national policy, was underway, nationalism in Croatia returned to the public arena. In March 1967, 17 leading cultural organizations in Croatia, including the literary society 'Matica Hrvatska,' published a manifesto demanding a change in the Constitution to provide better protection for the literary language of Yugoslavia, particularly the Croatian language. The document, *Declaration on the Name and Position of the Croatian Literary, Language* asked for an affirmation of Croatian national culture. The Declaration complained about the domination of the Serbian literary language as a state language, citing arguments and evidence that stirred up old emotions relating to the national question (Cohen & Warwick, 1983). Tito denounced the Declaration as a stab in the back of Yugoslav unity and declared the Novi Sad agreement on the 'Serbo-Croatian,' respectively 'Croato-Serbian,' language to be the best solution to the language problem (Hondius, 1968).

117

Despite Tito's intervention on the question of language, leading Croatian party leaders continued to demand greater autonomy and sovereignty for Croatia. The so-called mass movement (Maspok) became the driving force of Croatian nationalism. According to Marko Veselica (1980), one of the leaders of this movement, some of the principal aims of the Maspok were as follows:

(1) The transfer of the means of capital accumulation, i.e. of new investments, from the Federation, its banks and reexporting enterprises to the primary creators - to the basic units of production and their organizations, to the several nations and their republics.

(2) The Croatian democratic movement sought a drastic restructuring of the entire Federal decision-making mechanism. What we strove for, was that each nation's sovereignty be expressed within the framework of its own republic, that decisions be made democratically by the chosen representatives of each nation and that larger nations could not impose their will on the smaller ones. . . . Yugoslavia's common interest should represent the sum total of the needs and interests of the component republics.

(3) The Croatian democratic movement sought to create conditions in which it would be possible to write about Croatian history objectively, in which it would be possible to develop the Croatian language and properly preserve the Croatian national and historical inheritance. Various conquerors, unitarists and hegemonists have sought to deny the Croatian nation the right to its own identity. . . . We were criticized for glorifying Ante Starcevic, the founder of modern Croatian nationalism, who was systematically ignored and denigrated by the regime because he was an uncompromising defender of Croatian statehood. We were not even allowed to commemorate the tragic death of Stjepan Radic, the great Croatian tribune and political leader, who was murdered in the Belgrade parliament in 1928. (pp. 3-8)

Tito was at that time already concerned with the growing expression of nationalist sentiments by members of the intelligentsia in Croatia and some other regions of the country, and he recognized that such sentiments were tolerated and sometimes even encouraged by regional party leaders (Cohen & Warwick, 1983). He was particularly concerned with the intensity of the national question in Croatia which in his view threatened nothing less than a major political crisis verging on civil war (Vjesnik, in Cohen & Warwick, 1983).

Tito decided to take action. In early 1972, with the support of the military, he boldly engineered an extensive purge of the League of Communists in Croatia, expelling prominent party leaders and their associates accused of nationalist sentiments. Arrest and criminal prosecution followed (Cohen & Warwick, 1983). According to Sime Djodan (In Ramet, 1992), thousands of Croats were punished in one way or another. He estimates that 50,000 members of the League of the Communists of Croatia lost their party cards, 12,000 enterprise directors and engineers were fired, and 2,000 to 5,000 persons were imprisoned. Among those arrested and sentenced were Marko Veselica, Sime Djodan, and Franjo Tudjman. But the purge did not liquidate Croatian nationalism; it only drove it underground. This left only one institution available to champion Croatian national interests until 1989--the Croatian Catholic Church.

Political birth of the Moslim Nation and party intervention

The Fifth Congress of the League of Communists of Bosnia and Herzegovina (9-11 January, 1969) capped the process of recognition of the Moslem nation by formally endorsing its complete equality with the other Yugoslav nationalities. One of the major events in the political recognition of the Moslem nationality was its formal recognition on the 1971 census forms. In the 1948 census, Bosnia's Moslems had only three options: Serb-Moslem, Croat-Moslem, and ethnically undeclared Moslem. Moslim identity had been treated as a matter of religious preference rather than ethnicity in the 1953 census, but the category Yugoslav, ethnically undeclared, was introduced at that time (Ramet, 1992).

These events led Moslim nationalists to agitate for redesignating Bosnia as a Moslim republic in the same way that Serbia was the Republic of Serbs, and Macedonia the Republic of Macedonians. The Moslem nationalists wished the Bosnian Constitution to read something to the effect that the Socialist Republic of Bosnia-Herzegovina is a state based on the sovereignty of the Moslem nation; it is the national state of the Moslem nation and of the members of the Serbian and Croatian nations who live in it, as well as of the members of other nations and nationalities who live in it. At about the same time, some Bosnian linguists started the idea that Bosanski, the language of the Moslems, should be recognized as a distinct language in the Yugoslav state.

Increasing Moslim nationalism was recognized by the Communist Party as potentially threatening, and in 1972, two leading Moslim politicians, Avdo

Humo and Osman Karabegovic, were dismissed from their posts for alleged Moslem exclusivism and nationalism (Ramet, 1992).

The constitutional amendments of 18 April 1967

Despite the tough stance against nationalists and their demands for greater autonomy, the political leadership of Yugoslavia continued with decentralization of the country based on the principles of self-governance. Only four years old, the Constitution of 1963 was again subject to change; this time, change came in the form of constitutional amendments. These were not incorporated into but rather attached to the main text of the Constitution, similar to the amendments to the Constitution of the United States of America.

The most important changes concerning the national question came in April 1967 when the first of 41 amendments changed the system of election to the Chamber of Nationalities and broadened its rights and autonomy. The following year, with Amendment 8, the Federal Chamber was eliminated, and the Chamber of Nationalities became reconstructed as the Chamber of Delegates for the Republics and Autonomous Provinces, thereafter serving as the body with basic responsibility for legislation. In changes that followed, a demand for Kosovo and Vojvodina to be represented by their own delegations in the Chamber of Nationalities rather than through wings of the Serbian delegation was also accommodated (Hondius, 1968; Ramet, 1992).

The constitutional amendments were of far-reaching importance for the governmental structure of the country. Some Yugoslav scholars and politicians even argued that Yugoslavia was changing from a federation into a confederation. In 1971 Kardelj praised the new changes:

> Contemporary Yugoslavia is no longer a classic federation, nor can it be a classic confederation, but rather a socialist, self-managing community of nations, which to a great extent introduces simultaneously an essentially new category in inter-ethnic relations. The independence of nations in such a community grows greater than in classic federations and confederations, but, at the same time the processes of integration are opened wider in all areas where the common interest of the nations and working people is made manifest and where the conditions for equality are assured. (Sruk, in Ramet, 1992, p. 217)

120

Decentralization of League of Communists of Yugoslavia

Collective party leadership was introduced in 1969 at the League of Communists of the Yugoslavia Ninth Congress. The Executive Bureau of the Presidency was composed of 14 members - two from each republic and one from each of the two autonomous provinces. As a result of this and other restructuring, the League of Communists ceased to be a unified body. Ramet (1992) states that after 1969 there was no national communist party organization in Yugoslavia and that what unity the party had it owed to the unifying and commanding presence of Tito.

The League of Communists of Yugoslavia became a league comprising six republican and two provincial party organizations. After 1969, each of these eight regional parties held its own party conferences before rather than after the League of Communists of Yugoslavia Congresses.

Collective Presidency

The 23-member collective Presidency was the institutional embodiment of the principles underlying the amendments. It was composed according to the formula calling for equal representation of the Republics and corresponding representation of the Autonomous Provinces. It operated, however, on the basis of almost complete interregional political equality. Tito, as long as he remained President of the Republic, was to function as President of the Presidency (Burge, 1983, p. 217).

The Presidency was to include the Presidents of the Republican and Provincial Assemblies, two members elected by each of the Republican Assemblies, and one member elected by each of the Provincial Assemblies. Tito, as President of the Republic, also was to be a member. The decision on the Presidency's composition was consistent with the constitutional mandate, which required the Presidency to ensure the equality of the nations and nationalities (Burge, 1983, p. 207).

The 1974 Constitution

The ideological and political basis for a new constitution

The ideological basis for the draft of the 1974 Constitution was to be found in the reasonably elaborated form of the social theory developed in 1968 to 1971, especially through the affirmation and elaboration of the principle of self-management. The concept of self-management socialism as well as the concept

121

of self-management federalism could already be found in the Constitution of 1963 and in the amendments to that Constitution passed in the 1967 to 1971 period. It was also claimed by Yugoslav constitution-makers that the Constitution of the Swiss confederation and the U.S. Constitution inspired constructive solutions for Yugoslav federalism. The U.S. Constitution inspired the introduction and development of constitutionality and the rule of law as well as the mechanism for maintaining constitutionality within the scope of the Yugoslav Constitution (Djordjevic, 1988).

Djordjevic was the most well-known political scientist and authority on constitutional law in Serbia and Yugoslavia. He was reputed to have been the primary author, with Edvard Kardelj, of the 1963 Constitution (Burg, 1983, p. 211). The following objectives, according to Djordjevic (1988), were the basis for preparing the 1974 Constitution:

> (1) Strengthening the equality and community spirit of the nations (Serbian, Croatian, Slovenian, Macedonian, Montenegrin, and Moslem) and the nationalities (especially the Albanians and the Hungarians because of their large numbers);

> (2) Developing the concept of the socialist economic and social systems, founded on a Constitution of the Federal People's Republic of Yugoslavia, community ownership and worker self-management; and

> (3) Democratizing political processes and the political system as a whole.

Other issues were discussed and resolved in the same context, such as:

> (4) Broadening the rights of the Republics and decreasing the federation's jurisdiction compared with previous periods;

> (5) Transforming the previous autonomy of the regions of Vojvodina (due to its ethnic pluralism) and of Kosovo (as a result of the majority Albanian population) into autonomous provinces approaching the status of federal units; and

> (6) Introducing parallel heads of state, the Presidency of the Republic and the Presidency of Yugoslavia, with the stipulation that with the death of President Tito, all attributes of the head of state would be transferred to the Presidency of Yugoslavia as a collegial body. (pp. 185-6)

Djordjevic further emphasized that:

Yugoslavia is a multi-ethnic community made up of nations and groups that are, in the main, ethnically close but that differ in their interests, histories, and conditions of life. From this fact alone stems (1) the phenomenon of greater autonomy, yet greater unity, in the economic structure, the result of introducing the concept of the 'organization of associated labor' as an instrument to ensure the right of self-management in a direct manner; and (2) the degree of decentralization in the federal structure, which has led to the dilemma between confederalism and federalism. (p. 187)

Placement of Edvard Kardelj in the position of Chairman of the Constitutional Commission responsible for bringing a draft was considered by the Yugoslav leadership as the best way to protect the continuity of the Yugoslav experiment in self-management and decentralization.

Tito followed the work of the Constitutional Commission closely, giving his input on controversial questions. He supported introduction of the Presidency of Yugoslavia in addition to the office of the President of the Republic. Later he called for also consolidating the principle of collective decision making and the rotation of offices at all upper levels of the state (Djordjevic, 1988).

The Collective state Presidency

The 1974 Constitution had called for the Presidency to be composed of one representative from each of the Republics, the Provinces, and the Communist Party. This reduced the Presidency from 23 to 9 members. The smaller size, its increased authority, and the more federal character of the new Presidency made it potentially a more effective organ for the resolution of conflicts that could not be resolved in the other organs of the federation.

Under the 1974 Constitution, the function of the Presidency remained to realize the equality of the nations and nationalities and to achieve adjustments in the common interests of the regions. The Presidency continued to make decisions on the basis of the adjustment views and interests of the regions. Its rules of procedure provided for certain decisions to be adopted by a simple majority, while others required a two-thirds majority (Burg, 1983, p. 245).

The members of the Presidency, however, remained responsible to the Assemblies of their respective federal units, which in fact elected them, and therefore lacked a common vision (Ramet, 1992, p. 69).

The most radical changes incorporated in the 1974 Constitution concerned the organization and operation of the Federal Assembly. The Constitution defined the Assembly as being both the highest expression of the self-management system and the supreme organ of power within the framework of federal rights and duties. It was divided into two chambers: a Chamber of Republics and Provinces and a Federal Chamber. The Chamber of Republics and Provinces was the successor to the Chamber of Nationalities. The change of the name of this chamber also carried a symbolic meaning. The 'blocs' composing the Yugoslav system of interbloc negotiation were in this way defined as primarily territorial communities. Nationality would still be, and was, taken into account in the composition of certain institutions, but participation in those institutions was now to be defined in terms of territorial, not national, identity (Burge, 1983, pp. 250-1). Each of these territorial communities contained minority populations from ethnic groups other than the dominant group. Thus the problem of minority rights was transformed from the national to the republic levels of government.

The 1974 Constitution provided that the Chamber of Republic and Provinces was to be composed of 12 delegates elected by the Assembly of each Republic from among its own membership, and 8 were to be elected by the Assembly of each Autonomous Province from among its membership, for a total of 88 delegates. Individuals elected to the National Chamber were to retain their membership in their respective regional assemblies.

On issues subject to joint decision making by the regions, delegations were required to represent the positions of their respective assemblies. Decisions on such issues were considered adopted only when they had received the approval of each delegation. In effect, the regions were granted veto power over federal policies in areas subject to joint decision making.

The Chamber's rules of procedure stipulated that every delegation would have a chairman whose task it would be to represent their delegations in meetings of the leadership of the Chamber and in debates on the Chamber floor (Burg, 1983, p. 252). The delegations in the Chamber of Republics and Provinces (CRP) were responsible for coming to an agreement, since, except for emergency measures, all legislation required the unanimous agreement of every delegation. Before the process of mutual accommodation began in the CRP committees, however, the delegations met separately to review the positions of the other Republic and Provincial Assemblies. Once that was completed, the process of the harmonization of viewpoints began in earnest, advancing by means of compromise, alliance formation, and logrolling. The principle of unanimity took its toll in protracted negotiations in controversial areas (Ramet, 1992, p. 67).

The 1974 Constitution provided that the Federal Chamber should be composed of 30 delegates of self-managing organizations and communities and sociopolitical organizations from each Republic, and of 20 delegates from each Autonomous Province. Candidates for these positions were to be selected by the Socialist Alliance of Working People and elected by the commune assemblies of each region. Decisions in the Federal Chamber were to be made by a majority vote at sessions attended by a majority of delegates. The delegates to the Federal Chamber functioned as representatives of both the working class (organized into self-managing units) and organized socialist consciousness (embodied in sociopolitical organizations) (Burge, 1983, p. 255).

While the Chamber of Republics and Provinces was explicitly organized as an arena for interregional bargaining, the Federal Chamber was not. Delegates to the Federal Chamber were supposed to represent the views of the delegations from which they were elected independent of the influence of the Republic or Province in which those delegations were located. In practice, though, delegates to the Federal Chamber did not remain independent of such influence. In fact, shortly after the adoption of the 1974 Constitution, delegates to the Federal Chamber organized themselves informally into pseudodelegations paralleling the organization of the Chamber of Republics and Provinces (Burge, 1983, pp. 256-7).

Federalism and unity

Djordjevic (1988), in discussing the 1974 Constitution, argued that the text of the Constitution addressed the matter of unity and the unified federal structure:

> The federation was conceived and, in part, functions with the aim of realizing brotherhood and unity among national groups, a type of self-management in a democratic community. All endeavors to form national unity by older national groups are alien to the Constitution and to practice. This community, in its present stage and within the scope of the existing Constitution, honors the identity of the nations and, in equitable unity, permits the expression of national cultures and national particularities.

> The political system of Yugoslavia is ideologically and structurally centered on the federation. Yugoslavia is a federal state of united and associated nations and their Republics with specific autonomous provinces that together compose a type of federal unity to implement the principle of equality of nations and nationalities. This form of federalism is decentralized, with its sovereign basis in the nation, that is, in the republics as the nearest expression of that sovereignty,

bringing the republics closer to a constitutional definition as states. (pp. 192-3)

The author further argued that decentralized federalism had been established and was practiced in Yugoslavia. Some other authors also expressed their views on Yugoslav unity.

Pasic (1988), on the decentralization and cohesive forces that keep Yugoslavia together, elaborates as follows:

Self-management by definition means very far-reaching decentralization. Formerly centralized powers have been transferred partly to the workers of publicly owned enterprises and partly to territorial political centers, mainly in the republics and autonomous regions. The decentralization, however, did not always substantially reduce the influence of the government in economic matters. Many rights in these matters have simply been transferred from the central government to the governments of republics and autonomous regions. A new balance of forces has thus been established in the Yugoslav federation--this time in favor of the federal units.

People hoped that two cohesive forces would develop inside Yugoslav society. One was free economic integration on the basis of the self-managerial rights of workers, ensuring a free flow of labor and capital inside Yugoslavia. The other cohesive force was the social-political organizations which are organized partly on the basis of so-called democratic centralism. These two forces of cohesion should counterbalance the great individual powers of the republican states. The hopes for this cohesion have only partly been fulfilled, however, and that is why many problems persist in the functioning of the Yugoslav federation. (pp. 222-4)

Stanovcic (1988) addresses the same issues:

What were the basic features of the constitutional changes that took place from 1966 to 1974? In my view the changes had three aims. The first was to decrease the control of government over the economy and over worker self-management. This has not yet been successfully accomplished; although the federal government has lost power, the governments of the republics and provinces have strengthened their powers to the some degree.

The second aim of constitutional change was to reframe the Yugoslav federation. In my view we have gone too far in this respect. We have approached a system that could be properly be called a con-federation, because on most important questions all eight units have a veto power over the federal government. For a decision to be made, to change the Constitution, and so on, all eight have to agree. It is difficult to reach an agreement among them in the face of the religious, cultural, historical, and economic diversity of the country.

The third aim was to provide a constitutional solution for the problem of succession to power, especially since President Tito was the unchallenged leader for such a long time. This problem, in my view, has been satisfactorily solved; since Tito's death the government and the political system have continued to function normally. (pp. 224-6)

The Yugoslav Constitution of 1974 outlined the prerogatives, powers, and responsibilities of Yugoslav state formation as they were until the system disintegrated between 1989 and 1990. Despite the optimism of the creators of the 1974 Constitution as to the future of Yugoslavia, the death of Tito in 1980 had a significant impact upon the affected Yugoslav unity. The institutions of the 1974 Constitution were not capable of keeping the country together, despite the efforts to reform the economic and political system in the 1980's.

Conclusions

The First Yugoslavia was dismembered by Croats and neighboring states that had been awarded former Yugoslav lands for loyalty to Hitler and his expansionist policy. The Second Yugoslavia was created as a result of the defeat of Hitler and his puppets. The new international order after the Second World War brought back more or less the same territorial boundaries among the states that existed in the interwar period. But this time the world had become divided along the ideological cleavages of the Western democracies in opposition to Soviet Communism. The South Slavs found themselves again on the frontier of two worlds; as such, the new unified Yugoslavia looked to the international community as the only viable solution, since the idea of a separatist and independent Croatia had been discredited by the creation of the Fascist Croatian state during World War II.

Domestically, the partisan movement that had fought for the liberation of Yugoslavia from the Nazis and for the reintegration of the state did not have any competition. Originally started as a spontaneous resistance to occupation, the partisan movement emerged as the only force that gathered all South Slavs into a platform of national liberation and unification. The Communist Party led by Tito achieved a leadership position in the partisan movement, thereby allowing Tito and the Communist Party to add to the platform for liberation and unification another platform for changing the political system and discrediting the King and the interwar political establishment. What had been liberation war at the beginning became in the end a revolution, brought about by exploiting the sentiments of those South Slavs who had been victimized by the Nazis and their puppets. Tito deliberately diminished the horrors of the Croatian Fascists and their role in dismemberment of the First Yugoslavia. At the same time, he openly accused the King and his supporters of Serbian hegemony which, he said, caused the disintegration of the First Yugoslavia, and he further named the King and Serbs loyal to the King as the major obstacles to the South Slav reunification. It seems that Tito wanted to bring Croatia back into Yugoslavia by forgiving them their atrocities in the Second World War and by accusing Serbs for their closeness to the Monarchy.

The Second Yugoslavia was proclaimed on 29 November 1943 as a federation of peoples rather than a federation of ethnonational states. In order to gain the support of the Allies for his partisan movement, Tito did not insist on a declaration of the future form of the state. He prohibited the King from coming back, but he did not exclude monarchy as a possible future form of the state.

During the war, Tito's partisan movement was needed and supported by the Allies in order to fight Hitler's forces in the Balkans. It was a time when ideology did not matter. The Western democracies and the Soviet Communists fought in an alliance against the common enemy; everyone was welcomed to this cause. Tito played on that and won western and Soviet support, not only for the liberation of Yugoslavia but also for his concept of the Second Yugoslavia. At the end of the war, Yugoslavia's future was to be decided according to an international agreement by a Constituent Assembly. In the election for the Constituent Assembly Tito's People's Front was the only alternative on the ballot. The eventual opposition parties had already been defeated in the liberation war. There were no alternatives; both military and political power were firmly in the hands of one man and one party.

With peace, Tito wanted to build a new Yugoslav nation. In the process, as a Communist, he rejected in 1946 the democratic concepts of Western countries. Later, in 1948, he rejected Soviet totalitarian concepts of a proletarian dictatorship. After 1950, he used the concepts of self-management 'invented' by his closest associate, Slovene Edvard Kardelj, to experiment with the creation of a new Yugoslav nation and its nation-state. Given its history, there was no obvious means to build a Yugoslav nation and its nation-state. Tito faced a monumental task, and as can now be seen, only his personal stature and capability allowed the state to continue up until the time of his death.

The utopian nature of socialism and the socialist self-management ideologies made the process of nation-building dependent on continuing interpretations and reinterpretations of the socialist visions of how Yugoslav society should look. The Communist Party with its leadership was the only political institution formally entitled to formulate and interpret the concepts of a Yugoslav nation. Because, there was no consistency in the Communist Party definition of a Yugoslav nation. Yugoslavia was successively defined as the new nation, a community of peoples, a unified community of the Yugoslav working people, several nationalities with their distinct histories and commonality in socialist social relations, a socialist self-managing community of nations, and the like. This inconsistency in formulation and interpretation of the Yugoslav nation led to the endless adjustment of Yugoslav political and administrative institutions.

In the 1946 Constitution, the Yugoslav nation, like the Soviet Union, was defined as a union of nations that had already used their right to self-determination in the process of unification. Despite the rhetoric of a federation of the peoples, at a perceptual level the land was divided behind closed doors among Tito's associates and among top Communist party leaders into republics and autonomous units. Again, as was the case with the First Yugoslavia, the will of the people was not truly consulted. In 1946, Yugoslavia was divided, with boundaries of new units crossing the boundaries of ethnonations. Croats, Serbs, and Moslems sharednot only the land of a 'unified' Yugoslavia, but also the Republics of Croatia and Bosnia and Herzegovina. The Croats became a majority in their Republic, which incorporated Serbian Kraina (a former military frontier). In Bosnia and Herzegovina, the Serbs, Croats, and Moslems shared the land of the historic region of Bosnia and Herzegovina.

In the process of ethnic conflict management through constitutional engineering from 1946 to 1974, the Federation of Peoples become a Federation of Republics. Through the constitutional and political decentralization begun after the split with Stalin in 1948 and under the flag of socialist self-management, political power was gradually transferred from the center to the Republics. The increased political power of the Republics and the previously drawn territorial boundaries later become the basis for the disintegration of Yugoslavia. The 1974 Constitution institutionally and formally transformed the Yugoslav Federation into the Confederation of Yugoslav Republics.

The inability of the Communist party to formulate consistent concepts and to create an integrative political and administrative structure was compensated for by the strong authoritarian role of Tito and the Communist Party as ruler. Tito was not reluctant to use power and coercion in dealing with opposition, especially with the leadership of ethnic nationalism. It took 20 years for Croats to reemerge from silence and ask for greater autonomy and independence. The Croatian national movement ended with mass expulsion of its leaders from their positions of political power and with their imprisonment. The same, although on a much reduced scale, happened with Moslem nationalists in Bosnia and Herzegovina. From a perspective of ethnonational repression, the First and the Second Yugoslavia were not much different. Coercion and imprisonment of the political opposition's leadership that challenged the integrity of the Yugoslav state were used as the primary means of ethnic conflict management.

The major integrative role in the Second Yugoslavia was played by the Communist Party, which exercised its cohesive power through a principle of democratic centralism that demanded the membership to conform to the center. With the strong center that Tito provided, the Communist Party was able to maintain the integrity of Yugoslavia through the incorporation of its leadership and membership into political and administrative institutions. But with the decentralization of the Communist Party (collective leadership and strengthening of republican and provincial party organizations), the integrative power of the Communist Party was diminished. Decentralization in the Party was followed by decentralization in the political and administrative systems (collective presidency, the shift of power from the federation to the republics) through, as mentioned above, the changes in the Constitution in 1974.

Decentralization of the party and the political system was expected to contribute to the development of socialist man through the development of socialist self-management. Associations based on community ownership and worker self-management were expected to bridge the ethnic differences and territorial boundaries. There was, however, no evidence that the concept of socialist self-management could protect the unity of Yugoslavia. To the contrary, there was more evidence that the utopian nature of this concept along with the decentralization of the party and the political system were only leading to disintegration.

7 Yugoslavia after Tito and disintegration

The nation-building processes of the Second Yugoslavia were based on the inconsistent ideologies and visions of Tito and were expressed through the Communist Party. Inconsistency of vision was reflected in the many Constitutional revisions. The people of Yugoslavia had been continuously subjected to the ideology of brotherhood and unity of the socialist self-managing man from one side; at the same time, decentralization and disintegration of the political system's formal institutions hit them from the other side. The ideology of brotherhood and unity was kept alive only through the authoritarian rule of Tito and the principle of democratic centralism of the Communist Party. In 1980 Tito died, leaving Yugoslavia without a successor. The Communist Party's ability to keep the fiction of Yugoslav unity and to build new institutions for ethnic conflict management capable of replacing Tito's authoritarian rule were to be tested in the ensuing years.

In this chapter the failure of the Communist Party to transform Yugoslavia is analyzed, along with the major domestic and perceptual factors that led to Yugoslav disintegration after Tito's death. In addition, particular attention is given to changes in the international order at the beginning of the 1990s and the role of the international community in the final dismemberment of an already weakened Yugoslavia.

Tito's death and new leadership

The Constitution of 1974 invested each Yugoslav republic and province with theoretical 'statehood,' and it effectively created a semiconfederative political structure in which powerful sectional leadership emerged. Tito's death came during a period of growing centrifugal pressures generated by the authoritarian policies of Yugoslavia's regionally entrenched political elites. In place of the unified Communist Party elite that had dominated the political system after the Second World War, the regime in 1980 was characterized by six Republics and two provincial Communist elites who were able to utilize decentralized authority for their respective parochial interests (Cohen, 1993, p. 33). In addition, the disunified Communist elites had competition from former Communist - dissidents and non-Communist politicians who competed for the ethnonational space created with Tito's death.

Faced with an economic crisis and the interethnic bickering of the political elite during the mid-1980s, citizens throughout the country increasingly blamed Yugoslavia's ills on the post-Tito communist political establishment. This opened an opportunity for alternative ethnonationalistic leadership to emerge strongly in the political arena (Cohen, 1993, p. 47).

Imprisonment of Tudjman

Franjo Tudjman, as one of the leading figures of Croatian Spring at the beginning of the 1970s, was very critical of the overall developments of that decade. Despite the decentralization that came with the 1974 Constitution, Tudjman (1981) argued that the reestablishment of 'firm hand' rule and the reaffirmation of democratic centralism in the Communist government had not solved or even diminished the internal crisis; on the contrary, it had intensified it. He complained that neither the theoretical strengthening of the federation through the enactment of the 1974 Constitution, nor the establishment of the delegation system and the requirement that decisions be made through agreement among the Republics had as yet fundamentally altered the relationship between Belgrade and the Yugoslav Republics and Provinces. Nor had it led to the resolution of the constitutional issues relating to the federation (pp. 136-7). This political behavior is also recognized by Ramet (1992), who argues that the purge that followed the Croatian Spring and the closing of Matica Hrvatska could not end Croatian nationalism but it only drive it underground.

Tito's death was considered by major ethnonationalists as an opportunity to seize power by promoting anti-Yugoslav sentiments. Despite his death in the first half of the 1980s, the old regime continued to work through sheer inertia. By the end of 1980, Tudjman and his followers were once again taken to court. The charge was spreading anti-Yugoslav propaganda - that the Croatian people continued to be politically, economically, and culturally oppressed in socialist Yugoslavia. In February, Tudjman was sentenced to three years in prison (Ramet, 1992, p. 203). Again, imprisonment of Tudjman and his fellows couldn't eliminate Croatian nationalism; it just postponed the inevitable. Tudjman later reemerged as leader of the Croatian movement for independence and dismemberment of Yugoslavia.

Already in the late 1970s in Bosnia , a new generation of the Bosnian Moslems emerged and began to look to Islam as a basis for political mobilization. In response to political mobilization of the Moslems, the Yugoslav government reacted in the same way as it had in response to Croatian nationalist weakening. In April 1983, Yugoslav authorities uncovered an illegal organization of Bosnian Moslems working for the creation of an Islamic republic in Yugoslavia and having illegal ties with reactionary Moslems abroad. Eleven persons were put on trial and ultimately sentenced to prison for terms averaging more than eight years. They were given amnesty at the end of 1988. Among those sentenced was Alija Izetbegovic, whom the authorities had previously incarcerated in 1946 for Islamic fundamentalism (Ramet, 1992, pp. 185-6).

Despite imprisonment, Izetbegovic continued to work on his Islamic fundamentalist platform. His vision of the state and society and his political platform appeared again in 1990 in his book, *The Islamic Declaration*. (The book was reprinted by BOSNA, Sarajevo, in 1990.) The following are excerpts from this book:

> There can be no peace or coexistence between the 'Islamic faith' and non-Islamic societies and political institutions. . . . Therefore, there is no question of any civil principles, and the state should be an expression and should support the moral concepts of the religion. (p. 22)

> The Islamic movement should and must start taking over power as soon as it is morally and numerically strong enough to not only overthrow the existing non-Islamic, but also to build up a new Islamic authority. (p. 43)

> In one of the theses for an Islamic order today we have stated that it is a natural function of the Islamic order to gather all Moslims and Moslim communities throughout the world into one. Under present conditions, this desire means a struggle for creating a great Islamic federation from Morocco to Indonesia, from tropical Africa to central Asia. (p. 46)

> Pan-islamism always came from the very heart of the Moslem peoples. (p. 49)

Izetbegovic's uncompromising attitude toward the future vision of Bosnia elaborated in his book enlisted more and more supporters among Bosnian Moslems at the end of the 1980s and beginning of the 1990s. Toward the end of the 1980s, he reemerged, this time as exclusive leader of a secessionist movement in Bosnia and Herzegovina.

In search of a new constitution

In the years 1984 to 1987 the Yugoslav political establishment reached a general consensus that the political system was in crisis. The debate focused on amendments to the Constitution or the writing of a new constitution. That specified the need for democratization of the party and its political institutions (Ramet, 1992, p. 218). By 1986, the Yugoslav Presidency had agreed to authorize the preparation of amendments to the federal Constitution. On 21 January 1987, a coordinating group, headed by Hamdija Pozderac, came out with its preliminary proposal for minimal changes, including a proposal to create a unified legal system; to bring the railroad, postal, and telephone system under central authority; and to strengthen the unity of the Yugoslav economy - at the expense of the economic sovereignty of the individual Republics. This preliminary proposal immediately met strong opposition in some Republics. In Slovenia, the general reaction was outrage.

Despite the lack of national consensus, in August 1988 the draft amendments to the Constitution were published with the idea that they would be discussed, refined, and eventually passed. In Slovenia and Croatia, however, these amendments ran into trouble immediately (Ramet, 1992).

Crisis of the League of Communists and its disintegration

In 1989 the Communist leadership, faced with growing dissension as to the political future of Yugoslavia, recognized the need for immediate action. They recommended an extraordinary Congress as a way of dealing with the greatest crisis. It was agreed to hold the Fourteenth Extraordinary Party Congress in December 1989 - a date later postponed until January 1990. The Congress was supposed to tackle three areas: reform of the constitutional system, economic reform, and transformation of the League of Communists of Yugoslavia (Ramet, 1992, p. 224).

Despite the warning of the Slovenian Party leader Milan Kucan that the country was on the brink of civil war, there was some hope for a solution in the Congress. The draft program published in advance promised free multiparty elections, freedom of speech, guarantees for other human rights, and efforts to obtain entry into the European Economic Community. For the Slovenian party this was not adequate, and the Slovenian delegation walked out on January 23, causing the entire Congress to fall apart. The 'Congress of Salvation' ended in complete disarray. The Slovenian party wanted the entire League of Communists of Yugoslavia to be disbanded (Ramet, 1992, pp. 246-7).

An early warning by Johnson (1974) that only the Communist Party could keep Yugoslavia together was tested. He predicted that there were no foreseeable alternative political institutions, non- or anti-Communist, that could play this all-Yugoslav integrative role. The Communist Party failed. Johnson's expectations that weakening and dissolution of the League of Communists would permit a rampant increase in self-destructive nationalism was about to happen (pp. 2-3).

First multiparty elections

Disintegration and decline of the power of the League of Communists of Yugoslavia were followed by emergence of new political parties that captured the support of ethnonationalists. By early 1990, 86 such parties existed, - 31 in Croatia, 19 in Slovenia, 13 in Montenegro, 6 in Serbia, 6 in Kosovo, 6 in Vojvodina, 3 in Bosnia, and 2 in Macedonia (Ramet, 1992, p. 248). The number of parties increased rapidly throughout 1990.

Already in April 1990, the first multiparty elections took place in Slovenia and Croatia. In Slovenia the people split their votes, electing Milan Kucan, candidate of the rebel Communists, as President while giving the Demos, a coalition of parties that had campaigned on a platform of independence, control of the legislature. In Croatia the people elected Franjo Tudjman and his ethnonationalist Croatian Democratic Union. In July 1990 a referendum on the promulgation of a new constitution and multiparty system was held in Serbia and passed. In the elections that followed in December, Slobodan Milosevic and his Serbian Socialist Party won. In November 1990 multiparty elections took place in Bosnia, and the nationalist parties won (Moslem Party of Democratic Action (PDA), Croatian Democratic Union (CDU), Serbian Democratic Party (SDP)). The three national parties gained votes and seats almost directly proportional to individuals' choices of national identities in the 1981 census (the PDA, 33.8 percent; the SDP, 29.6 percent; and the CDU, 18,3 percent). They formed a grand coalition to defeat the reform Communists and Yugoslav Prime Minister Markovic's reformists on the second round, and agreed to govern in a trilateral power-sharing arrangement patterned after the federal government - a collective presidency of two members for each nation, and the like (Woodword, 1995, p. 122; Ramet, 1992, p. 248; Shoemaker, 1994, p. 312).

With the electoral victories of the ethnonationalist parties, the Yugoslav balance-of-power system was fundamentally changed. There was no more a political force to keep Yugoslavia together. Nor was there a political party that had the strength or desire to save Yugoslav unity.

Toward the final split

After the electoral victories of the ethnonationalist parties, the pressure of independence-minded Slovenia and Croatia continued, urging other Republics to dismantle the old federal structure of Yugoslavia. Serbia, on the other hand, applied pressure to protect the federal structure and unity of Yugoslavia. Slovenia and Croatia warned repeatedly that confederalization was the only formula under which a peaceful Yugoslavia could be preserved.

New Croatian Constitution

Croatia took the first step towards secession by promulgating the new Constitution of the Republic of Croatia on 22 December 1990. The Constitution resembled all the features of the idea of an ethnicnation and its state. Hayden (1992) recognizes such a phenomenon as constitutional nationalism, arguing that sovereignty of an ethnic nation requires a definition of its subject since only one entity may be sovereign. Constitutional nationalism establishes a nation as a bounded unity: a sovereign being with its own defining language, culture, and perhaps 'biological essence,' the uniqueness of which must be defended at any cost. Hayden goes to explain that this concept of nationalism was made explicit by Croatian President Franjo Tudjman in a theoretical treatise on nationalism published in English in 1981: 'Nations . . . grow up in a natural manner . . . as a result of the development of all those material and spiritual forces which, in a given area, shape the national being of individual nations on the basis of blood, linguistic and cultural kinship (p. 663).
  Following Tudjman's idea of the ethnic nation, the Croatian Constitution in its preamble refers to historical foundations:

> The millennial national identity of the Croatian nation and the continuity of its statehood, confirmed by the course of its entire historical experience in various statal forms and by the perpetuation and growth of the idea of one's own state, based on the Croatian nation's historical right to full sovereignty, manifested itself:
>
> -   in the formation of Croatian principalities in the seventh century;
> -   in the independent medieval state of Croatia founded in the ninth century;
> -   in the Kingdom of Croats established in the tenth century;

- in the preservation of the subjectivity of the Croatian state in the Croatian-Hungarian personal union;
- in the autonomous and sovereign decision of the Croatian Sabor of 1527 to elect a king from the Hapsburg dynasty;
- in the autonomous and sovereign decision of the Croatian Sabor to sign the Pragmatic sanction of 1712;
- in the conclusions of the Croatian Sabor of 1848 regarding the restoration of the integrity of the Triune Kingdom of Croatia under the power of the Ban, on the basis of the historical statal and natural right of the Croatian nation;
- in the Croato-Hungarian Compromise of 1868 regulating the relations between the Kingdom of Dalmatia, Croatia and Slavonia and the Kingdom of Hungary, on the basis of the legal traditions of both states and the Pragmatic sanction of 1712;
- in the decision of the Croatian Sabor of October 29, 1918, to dissolve state relations between Croatia and Austro-Hungary, and the simultaneous affiliation of independent Croatia, invoking its historical and natural rights as a nation, with the State of Slovenes, Croats and Serbs, proclaimed on the theretofore territory of the Hapsburg Monarchy;
- in the fact that the Croatian Sabor never sanctioned the decision of the National Council of the State of Slovenes, Croats and Serbs to unite with Serbia and Montenegro in the Kingdom of Serbs, Croats and Slovenes (December 1, 1918), subsequently (October 3, 1929) proclaimed the Kingdom of Yugoslavia;
- in the establishment of the Banovina of Croatia in 1939 by which Croatian state identity was restored in the Kingdom of Yugoslavia;
- in laying the foundations of state sovereignty during the Second World War, through decisions of the Antifascist Council of the National Liberation of Croatia (1943), as counter to the proclamation of the Independent State of Croatia (1941), and subsequently in the Constitution of the People's Republic of Croatia (1947), and several later constitutions of the Socialist Republic of Croatia (1963-1990).

At the historic turningpoint marked by the rejection of the Communist system and changes in the international order in Europe, the Croatian nation reaffirmed at the first democratic elections (1990) by its freely expressed will its millennial statehood and its resolution to establish the Republic of Croatia as a sovereign state. (Trifunovska, 1994, pp. 251-2)

Despite their millennial search for statehood, the Croats lacked an understanding or recognition of the other ethnic groups that had shared the same land with them for centuries, and of their right for identity, self-determination, and independence as well. The first article of the Constitutional basic provisions makes it clear that the Republic of Croatia is a unitary and indivisible democratic and social state. In creating a unitary state, the Croats found themselves with a form of state that they had fought against for so many centuries. They had even felt dominated in the federal state of Yugoslavia. Nevertheless, they did not offer the same similar autonomy to the ethnic groups that were living within the new Croatian state.

In Article 6, the Constitution established a basis for coercion and imprisonment of anyone who dared to challenge this unitary concept, stating: 'The work of any political party which by its programme or activity violently endangers the democratic constitutional order, independence, unity or territorial integrity of the Republic of Croatia shall be prohibited' (Trifunovska, 1994, pp. 251-2). By this provision the Croats ignored the parallel to the order they had fought against in their stateless history.

Secession of Slovenia and Croatia

In the first six months of 1991, the Yugoslav Republics tried to reconcile their differences. A number of conferences took place in an effort to find some formula to which all could agree. Slovenia and Croatia exerted additional pressure by threatening to secede on 26 June 1991 if no agreement could be reached on the framework for a new Yugoslavia. While negotiating a solution for Yugoslavia, Slovenia and Croatia were preparing for secession based on a plebiscite held on 23 December 1990 in Slovenia and a referendum held in May 1991 in Croatia. In Slovenia, approximately 88.5 percent of the citizens who turned out to vote expressed support for Slovenia's secession from Yugoslavia should that step be deemed necessary (Cohen, 1993, p. 176).

On 19 May 1991, the Croatian referendum on independence asked the question, 'Do you agree that the Republic of Croatia as a sovereign and independent state, which guarantees cultural autonomy and all civil rights to Serbs and members of other nationalities in Croatia, may enter into an alliance with other republics?' This choice was approved by 93 percent of the 83.6 percent of the electorate who chose to vote or, in total, 79 percent. Notwithstanding, the referendum was boycotted by most Serbs of the Krajina region, who had held their own referendum on May 12, approving overwhelmingly the decision to join the Republic of Serbia and to remain within Yugoslavia (Woodward, 1995, p. 143).

The threat of Croatia and Slovenia to secede was realized on 25 June 1991 - a day before the deadline. First Croatia and then Slovenia declared their secession from Yugoslavia. The Republic of Slovenia Assembly's Declaration of Independence reads as follows:

> On the basis of the right of the Slovene nation to self-determination, of the principles of international law and the Constitution of the former Socialist Federativ Republic of Yugoslavia and of the Republic of Slovenia, and on the basis of the absolute majority vote in the plebiscite held on December 23, 1990, the people of the Republic of Slovenia have decided to establish an independent state, the republic of Slovenia, which will no longer be a part of the Socialist Federative Republic of Yugoslavia. (Trifunovska, 1994, p. 288)

The Constitutional Decision on the Sovereignty and Independence of the Republic of Croatia states as follows:

> - Executing the will of the people as expressed at the referendum of May 19th, 1991,
>
> ... the Sabor of the Republic of Croatia enacts this
>
> Constitutional Decision on the Sovereignty and Independence of the Republic of Croatia.
>
> The Republic of Croatia is hereby proclaimed a sovereign and independent State. (Trifunovska, 1994, p. 300)

The Croatian Declaration on the establishment of the Sovereign and Independent Republic of Croatia reads as follows:

> The Sabor of the Republic of Croatia passes hereby the
>
> Declaration on the establishment of the Sovereign and Independent Republic of Croatia.
>
> I
>
> Proceeding from the thirteen centuries old state-law tradition on its territory between the Adriatic Sea and the river of Drava and Mura, the Croatian nation has preserved the consciousness of its identity and its right to identity and independence in the independent and sovereign State of Croatia.

Due to the coincidence of historical circumstances and to its position on the dividing line between Eastern and Western Christianity, of two frequently opposed civilizations and cultures with differing political, economic and other interests, the Croatian nation was throughout centuries compelled to defend its national state, simultaneously defending the nations living to the west of its territory.

. . .

The centralist, totalitarian system imposed by the Socialist Federal Republic of Yugoslavia hindered the Republic of Croatia from promoting and protecting its political, economic, cultural and other interests, which led to an increasing desire on the part of the Croatian people to disassociate themselves from the Yugoslav State.

. . .

IV

The Constitution[s] of the Federal People's Republic of Yugoslavia and the Socialist Federal Republic of Yugoslavia granted the Republic of Croatia the right to self-determination and secession. (Trifunovska, 1994, pp. 302-3)

In the same Declaration it is possible to recognize conflicting statements. The document accuses the former Yugoslavia of centralism and totalitarianism while the article that follows it is argues that the very same Yugoslavia granted the Republic of Croatia the right to self-determination. In fact, the principle of self-determination was never clearly defined. Croatia, of course, did not acknowledge such a right to the ethnic groups and nations with whom they had shared historic territory.

Civil War in Slovenia and Croatia

The Yugoslav People's Army (JNA) responded to the Declarations by sending troops into Slovenia (Ramet, 1992, p. 257). The war in Slovenia was short since the homogeneous character of the country made the war that ensued a war between the JNA and Slovenians, rather than a war between different ethnic groups. Through mediation by the European Community, agreement was reached on terms of disengagement, and the JNA troops were ordered to withdraw from Slovenia. As the war was short and the JNA withdrew from Slovenia, this gave the legitimacy to the Slovenian secession. Casualties in the Slovene-JNA war were relatively light on both sides. Only a dozen members of the Slovenian forces were killed and 144 were wounded; the equivalent figures for the JNA were 37 killed and 163 wounded (Cohen, 1993, p. 224).

By mid-July, however, a civil war started in the Krajina regions of Croatia populated by Serbs. Within a few weeks this war had escalated dramatically (Ramet, 1992, p. 257). The major difference between the war in Slovenia and the civil war in Croatia was in the character of the war: in Croatia it was rather a war between ethnic groups - ethnonations with opposing objectives. The Croats wanted to secede, while the Serbs (living in claimed Croatian territory) wanted to stay in Yugoslavia. Between July and December 1991, the Serbs, supported by the JNA, consolidated their control over almost one-third of the declared Croatian state in bitter warfare that resulted in high military and civilian casualties (an estimated 10,000 people killed and approximately 30,000 wounded) (Cohen, 1993, p. 225).

Reaction of international community and domestic response

The U.S. Secretary of State, James Baker, visited Yugoslavia on 22 June 1991, just a couple of days before Slovenia and Croatia declared their independence. He told the Republics that the United States favored Yugoslav unity and that it would not recognize the independence of Slovenia or Croatia. About the same time, it was announced by NATO that NATO did not consider Yugoslavia within its defense perimeter and therefore would not intervene in a Yugoslav civil war (Ramet, 1992, p. 253). Despite these warnings, Slovenia and Croatia proceeded with their declarations of independence.

When Croatia and Slovenia first declared their independence and the Yugoslav army struck in Slovenia, various countries repudiated the secessionist Republics and endorsed the continued existence of a unified Yugoslav state. Among the countries endorsing unity were the United States, the Soviet Union, China, Britain, France, Sweden, Denmark, Italy, Greece, Romania, Poland and (cautiously) Hungary. The governments of Austria and Germany, on the other hand, were broadly sympathetic to Croatian and Slovenian aspirations (Ramet, 1992, p. 265).

President George Bush immediately discouraged Slovenian and Croatian independence. On 26 June 1991, he expressed regret at the acts of secession, emphasizing that the United States planned to proceed as if Yugoslavia were still intact (Ramet, 1992, p. 257).

At a summit meeting on the island of Brioni on 8 July 1991, initiated by the European Community and presided over by the Dutch Foreign Minister, Hans van den Broek, an agreement was achieved on cessation of hostilities and a three-month moratorium on the implementation of Slovene (and Croatian) independence, but not on the declarations of independence themselves. The Brioni Agreement was hailed at the time as a triumph of European diplomacy (Silber & Little, 1995, pp. 180-2). This agreement was, however, only partially successful; it led to peaceful completion of secession only in Slovenia. Croatia, as a multiethnic society, was not able to share the benefits of the agreement with Slovenia. As elaborated above, a civil war escalated in Croatia despite the agreement.

Upon expiration of the agreement on October 7 and 8, Slovenia and Croatia respectively proceeded with independence without achieving prior mutual agreement with Yugoslav federal authorities. The Presidency of Yugoslavia reacted immediately, issuing its position concerning the proclamation of the independence of the Republics of Croatia and Slovenia on 11 October 1991 with the following statement:

> The Presidency of the SFR of Yugoslavia assessed and reiterates that the Republics of Slovenia and Croatia declared independence and sovereignty by unilateral unconstitutional acts that can not produce immediate constitutional-legal consequences. These acts constitute a flagrant violation of the territorial integrity of the SFR Yugoslavia and its State borders and as such are liable to all the consequences envisaged in the constitutional-legal system of the protection of the territorial integrity. (Trifunovska, 1994, p. 353)

Toward international recognition of the secessionist republics

Faced with an escalation of hostilities in Croatia and irreconcilable differences between Croatian, Slovenian, and federal authorities, Lord Carrington, President of the Conference on Yugoslavia of the European Community, on 20 November 1991, asked its Arbitration Committee (headed by Robert Badinter, the Chairman of France's constitutional court, which was attached to the Hague Conference on Yugoslavia) for an opinion on the legal status of Yugoslavia and the secessionist Republics.

The Arbitration Committee issued the following opinion:
   a) - Although the SFRY has until now retained its international personality, notably inside international organizations, the Republics have expressed their desire for independence;

   - in Slovenia, by a referendum in December 1990, followed by a declaration of independence on June 25th, 1991, which was suspended for three months and confirmed on October 8th, 1991;

   - in Croatia, by a referendum held in May 1991, followed by a declaration of independence on June 25th, 1991, which was suspended for three months and confirmed on October 8th, 1991;

- in Macedonia, by a referendum held in September 1991 in favor of a sovereign and independent Macedonia within an association of Yugoslav States;

- in Bosnia and Herzegovina, by a sovereignty resolution adopted by parliament on October 14th, 1991, whose validity has been contested by the Serbian community of the Republic of Bosnia and Herzegovina.

b) The composition and workings of the essential organs of the Federation, be they the Federal Presidency, the Federal Council, the Council of the Republics and the Provinces, the Federal Executive Council, the Constitutional Court or the Federal Army, no longer meet the criteria of participation and representativeness inherent in a federal State;

c) The recourse to force has led to armed conflict between the different elements of the Federation which has caused the death of thousands of people and wrought considerable destruction within a few months. The authorities of the Federation and the Republics have shown themselves to be powerless to enforce respect for the succeeding ceasefire agreements concluded under the auspices of the European Communities or the United Nations Organization.

3   Consequently, the Arbitration Committee is of the opinion:

- that the Socialist Federal Republic of Yugoslavia is in the process of dissolution;

- that it is incumbent upon the Republics to settle such problems of State succession as may arise from this process in keeping with the principles and rules of international law, with particular regard for human rights and the rights of peoples and minorities;

- that it is up to those Republics that so wish, to work together to form a new association endowed with the democratic institutions of their choice. (European Political Cooperation press release, 1991).

In mid-December 1991, Germany announced that it would recognize Slovenia and Croatia unconditionally on 15 January 1992. In response to the pressure from Germany, the European Community proceeded with steps to recognize independence-minded Republics. At the extraordinary European Community Ministerial Meeting held in Brussels on 16 December 1991, a Declaration concerning the conditions for recognition of new states was adopted. It was concluded that the Community and its member states would agree to recognize the independence of all the Yugoslav Republics fulfilling all the conditions set by the Community, and that the implementation of this decision would take place on 15 January 1992. They invited all the Yugoslav Republics to state by 23 December whether they wished to be recognized as independent states. The conditions and guidelines for Republics to be recognized were stipulated as follows:

> The Community and its member States confirm their attachment to the principles of the Helsinki Final Act and the Charter of Paris, in particular the principle of self-determination. They affirm their readiness to recognize, subject to the normal standards of international practice and the political realities in each case, these new States which, following the historical changes in the region, have constituted themselves on a democratic basis, have accepted the appropriate international obligations and have committed themselves in good faith to a peaceful process and to negotiations.
>
> Therefore, Community's common position on the process of recognition requires:
>
> - Respect for the provisions of the Charter of the United Nations and the commitments subscribed to in the Final Act of Helsinki and in the Charter of Paris, especially with regard to the rule of law, democracy and human rights;
>
> - Guarantees for the rights of ethnic and national groups and minorities in accordance with the commitments subscribed to in the framework of the CSCE;
>
> - Respect for the inviolability of all frontiers which can only be charged by peaceful means and by common agreement;
>
> - Acceptance of all relevant commitments with regard to disarmament and nuclear non-proliferation as well as to security and regional stability;
>
> - Commitment to settle by agreement, including where appropriate by resource to arbitration, all questions concerning State succession and regional disputes.

The Community and its member States will not recognize entities which are the result of aggression. They would take account of the effects of recognition on neighboring States. The commitment to these principles opens the way to recognition by the Community and its member States to the establishment of diplomatic relations. It could be laid down in agreements.

- They accept the provisions laid down in the draft Convention - especially those in Chapter II on human rights and rights of national or ethnic groups - under consideration by the Conference on Yugoslavia. (Trifunovska, 1994, pp. 431-2)

Again the Arbitration Committee was asked by Lord Carrington, Chairman of the Conference on Yugoslavia, for opinions concerning recognition of secessionist republics. On 15 January 1992, the Arbitration Committee submitted the following report:

The Arbitration Committee proceeded with an examination of this request by applying the provisions of the Declaration on Yugoslavia and the Guidelines on the Recognition of New States in Eastern Europe and the Soviet Union adopted by the EC Council of Ministers on December 16, 1991.

The Arbitration Committee has issued the following opinions:

Opinion No. 2 (The Right to Self-Determination)

1. The Committee considers that, at its present state of development, international law does not give a precise definition of all the consequences of the right to self-determination.

It is none the less well established that regardless of the circumstances, the right to self-determination cannot entail a modification of borders that are in place at the time of independence unless the states concerned reach an agreement to the contrary.
. . .

4. Therefore, the Arbitration Committee is of the opinion:

- that the Serbian populations of Bosnia-Herzegovina and Croatia have the right to enjoy all the minority and ethnic group rights recognized by international law and by the provisions of the Draft Agreement of the

145

Conference on Peace in Yugoslavia dated November 4, 1991, which the Republics of Bosnia-Herzegovina and Croatia have pledged to implement;

- that these Republics must enable the members of these minorities and ethnic groups to enjoy all the human rights and fundamental freedoms recognized, including, should the occasion arise, the right to choose their nationality.

Opinion No. 4 (Bosnia and Herzegovina)

. . .

4. In these circumstances, the Arbitration Committee is of the opinion that the expression of the will of the Bosnia-Herzegovina populations to constitute SRBH as a sovereign and independent state cannot be considered fully established.

The evaluation could be modified if guarantees were to be given in this respect by the Republic which would formulate the request for recognition, possibly by a referendum vote in which all the citizens of SRBH would participate, without discrimination and under international control.

Opinion No. 5 (Croatia)

- With this reserve, the Republic of Croatia fulfills the necessary conditions for recognition by the member states of the European Community according to the terms of the Declaration on Yugoslavia and the Guidelines regarding the recognition of new states in Eastern Europe and in the Soviet Union adopted by the EC Council of Ministers on December 16, 1991.

Opinion No. 7 (Slovenia)

. . .

4. As a result, the Arbitration Committee is of the opinion that the Republic of Slovenia satisfies the conditions set by the Guidelines regarding the recognition of new states in Eastern Europe and in the Soviet Union adopted by the EC Council of Ministers on December 16, 1991. (Report of ECAC, 1992)

The German government's public intention to recognize Croatia and Slovenia unconditionally undermined the mechanism agreed on by the European Council of Ministers to grant recognition only to those Republics that fulfilled certain criteria based on opinions provided by the Arbitration Committee. The Arbitration Committee, which published its findings the day before the German-led recognition, stated that   Slovenia had satisfied requirements of the Commission for independence but that the Commission had reservations concerning the recognition of Croatia because it had failed on two crucial points: first, Zagreb was not in control of all of its territory, and second, it had not provided sufficient guarantees for the protection of its minorities, most notably the urban Serbs who still lived in territory under Croatian control.

Despite these findings the German government persuaded members of the European Community to ignore the Commission's findings and to recognize both Slovenia and Croatia. In the other matter, the European Community reverted in the case of Bosnia and Herzegovina to the Arbitration opinion. The European Community told Izetbegovic that if Bosnia and Herzegovina held a referendum and a simple democratic majority assented to independence, then it would be granted. Requirements for all citizens to participate were dropped. As a result, Moslems and Croats were able to muster a majority by ignoring the principle of 'three constituent nations' (Gleny, 1994, pp. 163-4).

According to Gleny (1994), Izetbegovic was thus forced by German-led EC policy into the same mistake that Tudjman had made voluntarily; that is, he embarked upon secession from Yugoslavia without securing prior agreement from the Serbs (p. 164). As Gleny makes clear, the death sentence for Bosnia and Herzegovina was passed even earlier, in the middle of December 1991 when Germany announced that it would recognize Slovenia and Croatia unconditionally on 15 January 1992. In response to this German announcement, the former Secretary-General of the United Nation, Perez de Cuellar, wrote to Gensher, the Foreign Minister of Germany, urging Germany to reconsider its decision to recognize Croatia as this would provoke 'the most terrible war in Bosnia and Herzegovina.' This request was dismissed by Gensher, who wanted to recognize Croatia regardless of the cost to Bosnia (pp. 163-4).

Bosnia and Herzegovina and the road to civil war

Bosnia and Herzegovina, with its complicated mosaic of ethnoreligious communities (in 1991 it was 43.7 percent Moslem, 31.4 percent Serb, 17.3 percent Croat, and 5.5 percent Yugoslav), had long been recognized as one of the Balkan's most explosive powder kegs. By early February, 1992, relations among Bosnia's three major ethnic communities had significantly deteriorated. Ethnic leaders from the three communities had cooperated uneasily in the Republic's tripartite governing coalition since 1990, but spillover from the violence and animosity between Croats and Serbs in Croatia and growing uncertainty about Bosnia's future status and governance had raised ethnic tensions to a high pitch (Cohen, 1993, p. 236).

In the referendum recommended by the European Community held at the end of February 1992, Moslems and Croats voted overwhelmingly for Bosnia and Herzegovina's independence. Approximately 64.4 percent of the eligible voters cast votes, and 99.7 percent of the valid votes favored an independent Bosnian state. The Serbs, however, abstained from voting.

Ethnic violence in Bosnia was ignited on 1 March 1992, when an unidentified gunman fired on members of a Serbian wedding party who were waving Serbian flags in the mainly Moslem section of Sarajevo, killing the groom's father. Within hours, a dozen people were killed in the fighting that soon spread to other regions of the Republic (Cohen, 1993, p. 237).

Secession of Bosnia; response of the international community

The Hague conference on Yugoslavia was kept as a framework for separate talks on Bosnia and Herzegovina beginning in early February 1992 under the auspices of the European Community and its chair and chief negotiator, Jose Cutileiro from Portugal. Talks took place in Lisbon with the objective of finding a political settlement upon which the three-party leadership could agree in order to establish Bosnian stability and sovereignty. By the time of the Lisbon conference in March 1992, when violence had already started in Bosnia, all three parties spoke of ethnic cantonization of the Republic into three parts, something that would resemble Switzerland. The Lisbon agreement was signed on 18 March 1992, accepting the principles of the cantonization. President Izetbegovic had reneged within a week on his commitment to the document, and was supported immediately by the Croat leader Mate Boban. By late March, the Republic was at war (Woodword, 1995, pp. 280-1). In the events that followed, Bosnia and Herzegovina was recognized on 6 April 1992 by the United States and the European Community , eliminating the last hope of a comprehensive settlement that could prevent further war (Woodward, 1995, p. 283).

Declaration of a new Yugoslavia and the United Nations recognition of secessionist republics

The final official disintegration of Yugoslavia was completed by a Declaration of a new Yugoslavia, which was adopted by the remaining Republics of Serbia and Montenegro on 27 April 1992, and by recognition of the secessionist republics by the United Nations. The General Assembly Resolutions on Admission of Slovenia, Bosnia and Herzegovina, and Croatia to United Nations membership were adopted on 22 May 1992.

Conclusions

Establishment of a new Yugoslavia and the United Nations recognition of the secessionist Republics marked officially the end of an era of a unified South Slav state. There was no longer any political force with perceived benefits from a mutual society. Thus it appears that the fate of Yugoslavia was determined at its birth in 1918, though it took more than 70 years for domestic and international factors to create conditions for the final split. The ethnocentric nature of the self-management system contributed to the 'withering away' of the Yugoslav unified state by developing local and regional ethnic strongholds, and an inconsistent international community in the aftermath of the Cold War contributed further to the disintegration of Yugoslavia.

Tito's death in 1980 and the dissolution of the Communist Party by 1990 pushed the Second Yugoslavia into turmoil. Tito's successors were incapable of transforming Yugoslavia into a new multiparty democratic community. Instead, they turned to ethnonationalism using the memories of separate histories and identities of South Slav people for their own purposes. For the first time the South Slav people were asked what they wanted, and the answer was clear; they wanted their own ethnonational states, thereby requiring confrontation with the original Wilsonian questions from 1918: Who has the right to self-determination and their own state? Where are the boundaries of such states to be located? What is to happen to minorities within those states?

These questions are no longer simply those of a domestic nature. On the contrary, they represent urgent problems that need the force of a clear, orderly, and decisive set of principles developed by the international community for their solution. But to this day, the international community remains unclear and inconsistent, just as it was in 1918. The lack of clear principles may be traced to the balance of power contest that affected the character of the post-World War II international order. By the 1990s the two-power rivalry had vanished, making a clear definition of principles not only necessary but urgent. In the absence of such principles, Germany for the first time after the Second World

War exercised its power in pushing for a dismembering solution in the case of Yugoslavia. The United States, with its domestic political concerns, at the beginning left Europe to lead while advocating Yugoslav unity.

The lack of international principles and the increased fighting and carnage, at first in Croatia and then Bosnia and Herzegovina, pushed the international community to take part in making decisions. It sided with Germany in the recognition of Yugoslav dismemberment. Yet, what was recognized? It was the dismemberment of a multiethnic Yugoslavia and in its place the creation of a multi-ethnic Croatia and Bosnia and Herzegovina. Again, the nations did not coincide with the states. Croat and Moslem rights for self-determination were recognized, while the same rights were denied to the Serbs. The boundaries of the former Republics, drawn by Tito and his associates, were recognized as the boundaries of newly independent states. The multiethnicity of Yugoslavia was denied, while the same multiethnicity was, defacto, recognized in the new states.

From existing documents it is not clear that the nations recognizing the new state were fully aware of their multiethnic character or the problems that would arise from the newly created and fearful minorities within those states. Today (1997), in their concern to bring lasting peace to the region it is still not clear if they fully understand the nature of the problems that have been created.

8 Summary and conclusions

Ethnic conflict and violence

Ethnic conflict in the aftermath of the Cold War has become one of the most important social and political phenomena present in almost all societies. It was expected that modernization and democratization processes would lead to greater integration of ethnic groups in multiethnic societies. It was also expected that modern nationalism and nation-building processes following the French Revolution would bring freedom and sovereignty to all people regardless of their ethnic backgrounds.

For most of this century ethnic conflict remained relatively quiescent as a potential source of violence, and of intra- and interstate wars. Nation-states were recognized as legitimate and sovereign members of the international community; their territorial integrity was recognized and protected by international law and principles of noninterference in internal matters of other countries. Ethnic conflict was considered an internal matter of the respective countries, whose duty it was to manage ethnic conflict peacefully. Nation-states used many different methods in managing ethnic differences and accommodating claims of ethnonational movements. Most nation-states had been successful in ethnic conflict management due to the prevailing civic character of their societies, where accommodation, tolerance, and respect were major rules of the political game.

Prevailing scholarship on nations, nation-states, and ethnic conflict

Western democracies considered concepts of nations and nation-states as major conditions for the stability of the greater society. It was assumed that these concepts by themselves provided a necessary consensus on political institutions and the administrative state, which in turn preserved the stability of the greater society. However, some countries, such as those in Eastern Europe and the Balkans, despite the rhetoric of national unity, created political and administrative systems that severely polarized ethnic groups within the society. Only a strong authority in the form of political leadership, the Communist Party, or military control was able to keep these countries together.

It is questionable whether the international and domestic policies that were developed, based on western assumptions and theories of nation-states, were at all capable of finding solutions for such societies and states as Yugoslavia. Lack of a real sense of belonging to the same nation was not recognized, and this lack was even ignored in countries like Yugoslavia throughout this century. That is why the 'death' of Yugoslavia may be considered as the death of an impossible product of scholarship and social experimentation rather than the death of a nation. A nation that never existed cannot die. Only the assumption that Yugoslavia was a nation can die.

Throughout this century there was no sound theory of international relations that recognized the impossibility of creating a stable international community without recognizing differences in assumptions upon which particular societies integrate themselves into a greater society. Significant differences between civic and ethnic concepts of nations deserved more attention in scholarship and practices of the international order. The major assumption of the civic concept of nations is its inclusiveness of ethnic diversity, while the major assumption of the ethnic concept of nation is its exclusiveness, which could easily be used by ethnonationalists in their fight for ethnic purity. The idea of belonging to one nation by choice has been in permanent conflict with the idea of connectedness by blood and kinship. This major difference has not been recognized in the creation of nation-states and the international order throughout the twentieth century. Permanent ethnic bickering and recent ethnic violence and disintegration of some 'nations to be' have refuted the prevailing practical theory of the nation-state and the international order.

Once, when Yugoslavia and other socialist countries tried to transform their societies to multiparty democracies, the ethnonational skeleton of political and administrative institutions reemerged at the surface of political competition. As a result, some countries disintegrated peacefully, while others experienced ethnic violence. The worst case scenario happened in Yugoslavia; in recent years the country has undergone ethnic violence, civil war, and disintegration.

Model for comparative study of ethnic conflict

In this study I developed a model that can be used comparatively to identify and analyze conditions most likely to be related to ethnic violence and subsequent national disintegration. In this model, ethnic conflict is regarded as a dependent variable of domestic, international, perceptual, and systemic independent variables. I attempted to explain the ethnic violence and disintegration of Yugoslavia, aiming to highlight some unrecognized perceptual, domestic, and international conditions that may be in causal relationship with the worst case scenario. In my search for answers, I argued that the process of socialist self-management development contributed to extreme decentralization and subsequently disintegration of the Yugoslav political and administrative institutions on the basis of ethnic identity, leading to extreme ethnonationalism, violence, and civil war. At the same time, I also demonstrated that violence and disintegration would have been less likely to occur had the international community been more consistent in asserting policies and principles on which world order and the recognition of new states were to be established.

I expect this study to help domestic and international policymakers to better understand the background of ethnic violence and disintegration in Yugoslavia, and subsequently to develop a policy that can lead to a long-term peaceful solution in that country, as well as to prevent similar events in other countries.

Yugoslavia - Nation to be

The First Yugoslavia

The First Yugoslavia resembled a big laboratory for social, political, and administrative engineering. The objective of the experiment was to test whether a constitutional monarchy and a unitary state could provide South Slavs with an institutional framework that could peacefully reconcile and accommodate their historic differences.

Yugoslavia was created in 1918 as the Kingdom of the Serbs, Croats and Slovenes. The perception that all South Slavs are the same people and should live in the same nation-state was created on an assumption that they are of the same blood and kinship. At the very beginning of the process of the state's creation, the 'people' were not asked whether they shared this perception with the advocates of the idea of a mutual state. The idea of a constitutional monarchy and a unitary state was challenged immediately at the time of creation by the Croats, who expressed strong opposition to a common state in the first elections. In these they voted almost exclusively for the ethnically based Croatian Party. In addition, for the entire life of the First Yugoslavia, Croatian political leadership used ethnic mobilization as their primary source of political power. Croatian political behavior and permanent claims for self-determination and secession pushed them into permanent conflict with the Serbs, who had been divided along political preferences of radicals or democrats. Imprisonment of the Croatian political secessionist leadership was not sufficient to solve the problem; this only temporarily silenced Croatian claims for secession. In the 1929, constant bickering and fighting of Croats and Serbs led to violence in the Parliament and to King Alexander's decision to suspend the Parliament and assume personal rule. Personal rule was abandoned two years later with the introduction of Guided Democracy.

The change of the country's name to the Kingdom of Yugoslavia in 1929, and additional efforts by King Alexander to present himself as the King of all South Slavs were not able to promote greater national unity among the South Slavs. Territorial administrative division into nine 'banovinas,' announced with the change of the Kingdom's name, in an effort to provide some autonomy for the nine regions, initiated the first step toward decentralization of a unitary state.

The rise of Fascism in Germany was seen as an opportunity by Croatian ethnonationalists to achieve their goals. Initially they used the threat of Fascism as their means to extend Croatian territorial boundaries within Yugoslavia. With the German invasion of Yugoslavia, however, Croatian ethnonationalists seized the opportunity to create a fascist puppet Independent State of Croatia. Moreover, in the name of ethnic purity, their state conducted massive slaughtering of Serbian, Jewish, and Gypsy populations living within the boundaries of their newly created fascist state.

In the First Yugoslavia there was no evidence that a Yugoslav nation had been built. Much more in evidence was the fact that the Yugoslav experiment contradicted dominant Western scholarship and practice on nation-states and international order. Lack of national unity of South Slavs, burdened by different histories and perceptions of separate nationhood and statehood in extreme conditions, such as emergence of Fascism in Europe, contributed to the dismemberment of the First Yugoslavia - which was never a viable nation in the first place.

The Second Yugoslavia

With the fall of Fascism and the victory of the partisan resistance movement, the idea of a unified Yugoslavia got its second chance. The Yalta Conference approved creation of the new Yugoslav state. Again, historical differences of the South Slavs were ignored in favor of the already failed assumption of Yugoslavia as a nation-state. This time Yugoslavia was recognized under the leadership of Tito and the Communist Party. Although Tito and his associates in their addresses to the people featured Yugoslavia as a union of nations, they still divided Yugoslavia into six republics and two provinces. As a metter of fact, at the time the Second Yugoslavia was created, they established territorial bases that set the stage for dismemberment in the 1990s. Tito and his associates created boundaries for the Republics that had never existed before; this was done behind closed doors without consent of the people. Newly created territories of the Republics included intermingled populations of South Slavs, particularly in Bosnia and Croatia. The Republics needed only decentralization and revival of ethnonationalism to become ethno-national-states.

The process of decentralization started with the introduction of the socialist self-management system in 1950. Through permanent constitutional engineering over the years, under the banner of decentralization, ethnonationalistic forces were gradually gaining ground in their Republics. Gradually, political power was shifted from the center to the periphery, with the result that Yugoslavia unofficially became a confederation of nation-states with the introduction of the 1974 Constitution.

Disintegration

The only forces that kept Yugoslavia together were Tito and the Communist Party. Tito died in 1980, and the Communist party dissolved itself in 1990. The process of transition toward a multiparty democracy caught Yugoslavia with an extremely weak central authority, disintegrated political and administrative institutions, and no serious political party with a Yugoslav platform. For this reason, the inherited Yugoslav political institutions and administrative state appeared incapable of maintaining unity in the absence of a strong central authority. It was the system of socialist self-management that generated such ethnic polarization of South Slavs.

The South Slavs, affected by the long process of self-management, followed by national disintegration, could not articulate mutual interests and organized themselves into political parties across ethnic boundaries. Therefore, the one-party system was replaced by the multi-ethno-national-party system, and that was used by extreme ethnonational leaders to dismember Yugoslavia. The price was ethnic violence and civil war.

The international community, after failing to recognize the signs of potential disaster, only added fuel to the fire. Instead of providing Yugoslavia with the necessary assistance and time for democratization and a negotiated settlement, it played the power game, allowing individual countries to exercise their muscle in creating a New World Order. Failing to revisit the major nation-state and international order paradigms (regionally associated with strong state nationalism) in order to provide revised principles and decisiveness, the international community reacted instead with compromises and indecisiveness and by dividing and aligning along the ethnic lines of Yugoslavia. As a consequence, the ethnic cleavages of Yugoslavia became the ethnic cleavages of the world. Germany sided with the Croats, extremists from the World of Islam sided with the Moslems, and the rest of the world was not much interested. The power game ended with support for dismemberment along Tito's arbitrary territorial boundaries that had never existed in history before his time, particularly in multiethnic Bosnia. The international community awarded the right of self-determination to the Croats and Moslems within those territories, while the Serbs found that the same rights were denied to them as residents in those lands. This was a New World Order that divided Balkan communities along lines that neglected historically complex mixes of ethnic groups, leading, in turn, to extreme efforts, including ethnic cleansing, because such complexities had been ignored.

Recommendations

My chief recommendation to international policymakers is to follow the scenario of the Carter Center of Emory University, which includes gaining an understanding of the background of the conflict and barriers to peace, followed by the development of strategies and actions to resolve the conflict. The development of appropriate policy measures requires relevant diagnosis and revisitation of prevailing practical theories of nation-states and the international order . Similarly, the potential sources of ethnic violence should be identified rather than ignored, and the policy measures should be clear and consistent based on universal principles. With respect to international policy failure to stop the ethnic violence in Yugoslavia and potential lessons to prevent similar conflicts elsewhere, my questions are: (1) Would it not have been better for the international community to send assistance to all ethnonational parties in order to expose the membership to rules of tolerance, accommodation, and respect as well as to democratic political institutions in other countries having a record of successful ethnic conflict management, than to send the United Nations and NATO military power to separate already divided parties? (2) Would it not have been better to push the leadership of all parties to sit and negotiate at the same table, guided with clearly defined principles of self-determination and secession that would recognize the deficiencies of prevailing theories of nation-states and international order, than to meet each party separately advocating their extreme positions? Clearly, the answers today should be in favor of a peaceful solution; the tragedy that has unfolded demonstrates the folly of earlier theories and actions.

Additionally, further research should focus on a more effective way to deal with self-determination and recognition of new states. In order to highlight the specifics of ethnonational questions in different countries, comparative studies should be conducted of the Yugoslav experience with the experience of the former Czechoslovakia, the former Soviet Union, and such emerging states as Georgia, Armenia, Azerbaijan, and other countries in transition, as well as countries like South Africa, Zimbabwe, Rwanda, and Mozambique. Also, further research could be conducted on the specifics of the Kurd's national problem - as the case of a nation without its own state, and the Hungarian national problem - as the case of a nation that peacefully lives in its own state, as they do in the neighboring states of Slovakia, Romania, Yugoslavia, Croatia, and Austria. Again, comparative studies should be conducted on countries with consociational democracies (Switzerland, Belgium, Netherlands) that have managed to keep the country together despite decentralization. Political institutions and policies of decentralization in specific countries should be analyzed and compared in the context of ethnic conflict.

Bibliography

Adizes, Ichak (1971), *Industrial Democracy: Yugoslav Style - The Effect of Decentralization on Organizational Behavior*, The Free Press: New York.

Adizes, Ichak (1975), *Research Paper: The Developing Nations and Self-Management*, University of California Los Angeles, Institute of Industrial Relations: Los Angeles.

Adizes, Ichak and Borgese, Elisabeth Mann (eds.) (1975), *Self-Management: New Dimensions for Democracy*, ABC - Clio Press: Santa Barbara, CA.

Albrecht, Ulrich and Forsberg, Randall (1995), 'Security in the New Era:New Challenges, Long-term Goals, and Transitional Regimes', Third Draft Paper prepared for the International Fighter Study.

Alderman, Geoffrey (ed.) (1993), *Governments, Ethnic Groups and Political Representation, Comparative Studies on Governments and Non-Dominant Ethnic Groups in Europe, 1850-1940*, New York University Press: New York.

Anderson, Benedict (1991), *Imagined Communities, Reflections on the Origin and Spread of Nationalism*, Verso: London.

Anderson, Charles W. (1977), *Statecraft: An Introduction to Political Choice and Judgement*, Wiley: New York.

Arend, Anthony Clark and Beck, Robert J. (1993), *International Law and the Use of Force, Beyond the UN Chapter Paradigm*, Routledge: London.

Asmerom, Haile K. (1994), 'Democratization and the Neutrality of Public Bureaucracy in Multiethnic Societies: The Case of Ethiopia', Paper presented at Amsterdam Round Table Conference on The Impact of the Democratization Process on the Neutrality of Public Bureaucracies in Eastern Europe and in Third World Counties.

Banac, Ivo (1984), *The National Question in Yugoslavia*, Cornell University Press: Ithaca.

Basch, Linda, Schiller, Nina Glick and Blanc, Cristina Szanton (1994), *Nations Unbound*, Gordon and Breach Science Publishers: Langhorne, PA.

Beard, Charles A. and Radin, George (1929), *The Balkan Pivot: Yugoslavia, A Study in Government and Administration*, Macmillan: New York.

Bell, Wendell and Freeman, Walter E. (eds.) (1974), *Ethnicity and Nation-Building: Comparative, International and Historical Perspectives*, SAGE Publications: Beverly Hills.

Brass, Paul, ed. (1985), *Ethnic Groups and the State*, Barnes: Totowa, NJ.

Breuilly, John (1982), *Nationalism and the State*, St. Martin's Press: New York.

Breuilly, John (1994), *Nations and the State*, The University of Chicago Press: Chicago.

Brown, Michael E. (ed.) (1993), *Ethnic Conflict and International Security*, Princeton University Press: Princeton, NJ.

Brown, Seyom (1994), *The Causes and Prevention of War*, St. Martin's Press: New York.

Brubaker, Rogers (1994), 'Nationhood and the National Question in the Soviet Union and Post-Soviet Eurasia: An Institutionalist Account', *Theory and Society*, 23, pp. 47-72.

Buchheit, Lee C. (1978), *Secession, The Legitimacy of Self-Determination*, Yale University Press: New Haven

Bugajski, Janusz (1994), *Ethnic Politics in Eastern Europe*, M. E. Sharpe: Armonk, NY.

Burg, Steven L. (1983), *Conflict and Cohesion in Socialist Yugoslavia, Political Decision Making Since 1966*, Princeton University Press: Princeton, NJ.

Caiden, Gerald E. (1966), *Administrative Reform*, Aldine: Chicago.

Caiden, Gerald E. (1970), *Israel's Administrative Culture*, Institute of Governmental Studies: Berkeley.

Caiden, Gerald E. (1975), *The Myth of Depolitization: Reflections on a Dominant Party Competitive System*, SICA (Section on International and Comparative Administration, American Society for Public Administration) Occasional Paper: Hayward, CA.

Caiden, Gerald E. (1993), 'Decentralization in the Context of Institutionalizing Administrative Reform', University of Southern California, Class Paper: Los Angeles.

Caiden, Gerald E. (1993), 'Globalizing the Theory and Practice of Public Administration', University of Southern California, Class Paper: Los Angeles.

Caiden, Gerald E. and Caiden, Naomi (1995), 'Brothers' Keepers', *Society*, Vol. 32, No. 6, pp. 16-22.

Cerovic, Bozidar (1991), *Od Nacionalizacije do Privatizacije*, Ekonomcki Fakultet: Beograd.

Chauhan, Shivdan Singh (1976), *Nationalities Question in USA and USSR, A Comparative Study*, Author: New Delhi, India.

Cleveland, Harlan (1993), *Birth of a New World, An Open Moment for International Leadership*, Jossey-Bass: San Francico.

Cohen, Lenard and Warwick, Paul (1983), *Political Cohesion in a Fragile Mosaic, The Yugoslav Experience*, Westview Press: Boulder, CO.

Comaroff, John L. and Stern, Paul C. (1994), 'New Perspectives on Nationalism and War.' *Theory and Society*, 23, pp. 35-45.

Connor, Walker (1984), *The National Question in Marxist-Leninist Theory and Strategy*, Princeton University Press: Princeton, NJ.

Connor, Walker (1994), *Ethnonationalism, The Quest for Understanding*, Princeton University Press: Princeton, NJ.

Constitution of the Federative People's Republic of Yugoslavia, 1947.

Constitution of the Federal People's Republic of Yugoslavia, 1960.

Cozic, Charles P. (1994), *Nationalism and Ethnic Conflict*, Greenhaven Press: San Diego.

Croatian National Congress (1988), *The Croatian Response to the Serbian National Program*, The Croatian National Congress: Saddle River, NJ.

Crossette, Barbara (1994), 'What is a Nation?', *The New York Times*, December 26, p. Y 5.

Dahl, Rober A. (1971), *Polyarchy: Participation and Opposition*, Yale University Press: New Haven.

Davis, Lynn E. (1993), *Peacekeeping and Peacemaking After the Cold War*, Rand Summer Institute: Santa Monica, CA.

Dawisha, Karen and Parrott, Bruce (1994), *Russia and the New States of Eurasia, The Politics of Upheaval*, Cambridge University Press: Cambridge.

Denitch, Bogdan (1990), *Limits and Possibilities,The Crises of Yugoslav Socialism and State Socialism Systems*, University of Minnesota Press: Minneapolis.

Denitch, Bogdan (1994), *Ethnic Nationalism, The Tragic Death of Yugoslavia*, University of Minnesota Press: Minneapolis.

Deutch, Karl (1966), *Nationalism and Social Communication: An Inquiry into the Foundations of Nationality*, M.I.T. Press: Cambridge, Mass.

Diamond, Larry and Plattner, Marc F. (eds.) (1994), *Nationalism, Ethnic Conflict, and Democracy*, The Johns Hopkins University Press: Baltimore.

Djilas, Aleksa (1991), *The Contested Country, Yugoslav Unity and Communist Revolution, 1919-1953*, Harvard University Press: Cambridge, MA.

Djilas, Milovan (1982), *Tito, koj drug, i moj vrag*, Lev: Paris.

Djordjevic, Jovan (1984), *Socijalizam kriza odgovornosti: deset ogleda o otvorenim pitanjima drustveno-politickog i pravnog sistema*, Radnicka stampa: Beograd.

Djordjevic, Jovan (1988), 'The Creation of the 1974 Constitution of the Socialist Federal Republic of Yugoslavia', In Goldwin, Robert A. and Kaufman, Art (eds.), *Constitution Makers on Constitution Making*, American Enterprise Institute: Washington, D.C., pp. 184-209.

Donia, Robert J. and Fine, John V. A. Jr. (1994), *Bosnia and Hercegovina: A Tradition Betrayed*, Columbia University Press: New York.

Dragnich, Alex N. (1978), *The Development of Parliamentary Government in Serbia*, East European Quarterly: Boulder, CO.

Dragnich, Alex N. (1983), *The First Yugoslavia, Search for a Viable Political System*, Hoover Institution Press: Stanford, CA.

Dragnich, Alex N. (1992), *Serbs and Croats, The Struggle in Yugoslavia*, Harcourt Brace Jovanovich: New York.

Duncan, Raymond W. and Holman, G. Paul Jr. (eds.) (1994), *Ethnic Nationalism and Regional Conflict, The Former Soviet Union and Yugoslavia*, Westview Press: Boulder, CO.

Eckstein, Harry (1966), *Division and Cohesion in Democracy*, Princeton University Press: Princeton, NJ.

Enloe, Cynthia H. (1973), *Ethnic Conflict and Political Development*, Little, Brown and Company: Boston.

Esman, Milton J. (1994), *Ethnic Politics*, Cornell University Press: Ithaca, NY.

European Political Cooperation Press Release (1991), *Declaration on Yugoslavia*, December 7.

Evans, Gareth (1993), *Cooperating for Peace, The Global Agenda for the 1990s and Beyond*, Allen & Unwin: St Leonards, Australia.

Farazmand, Ali (ed.) (1991), *Handbook of Comparative and Development Public Administration*, Dekker: New York.

Farley, Lawrence T. (1986), *Plebiscites and Sovereignty, The Crisis of Political Illegitimacy*, Westview Press: Boulder, CO.

Fassmann, Heinz and Munz, Rainer (eds.) (1994), *European Migration in the Late Twentieth Century*, International Institute for Applied Systems Analysis: Laxenburg, Austria.

Fisher, Jack C. (1966), *Yugoslavia- A Multinational State, Regional Difference and Administrative Response*, Chandler: San Francisco.

Gable, Richard W. (1976), *Development Administration: Background, Terms, Concepts, Theories, and a New Approach*, SICA (Section on International and Comparative Administration, American Society for Public Administration) Occasional Paper: Hayward, CA.

Garber, Larry and Bjornlund, Eric (eds.) (1992), *The New Democratic Frontier, A Country by Country Report on Elections in Central and Eastern Europe*. National Democratic Institute for International Affairs: Washington, D.C.

Gellner, Ernest (1983), *Nations and Nationalism*, Cornell University Press: Ithaca, NY.

Glenny, Misha (1994), *The Fall of Yugoslavia, The Third Balkan War*, Penguin Books: New York.

Glenny, Misha (1995), 'The Age of the Parastate', *The New Yorker*, May 8, pp. 45-53

Goertz, Gary and Diehl, Paul F. (1992), *Territorial Changes and International Conflict*, Routledge: New York.

Goldmann, Robert B. and Wilson A. Jeyaratnam (eds.) (1984), *From Independence to Statehood, Managing Ethnic Conflict in Five African and Asian States*, St. Martin's Press: New York.

Gotlieb, Gidon (1993), *Nation Against State, A New Approach to Ethnic Conflicts and the Decline of Sovereignty*, Council of Foreign Relations Press: New York.

Greenfeld, Liah and Chirot, Daniel (1994), 'Nationalism and Aggression.' *Theory and Society* 23, pp. 79-130.

Griffiths, Stephen Iwan (1993), *Nationalism and Ethnic Conflict, Threats to European Security*, SIPRI (Stockholm International Peace Research Institute) Research Report No. 5, Oxford University Press: New York.

Gupta, Dipankar (ed.) (1992), *Social Stratification*, Oxford University Press: Oxford.

Gurr, Ted Robert (1993), *Minorities at Risk*, United States Institute of Peace Press: Washington, D.C.

Gurr, Ted Robert and Harf, Barbara (1994), *Ethnic Conflict in World Politics*, Westview Press: Boulder, CO.

Haass, Richard N. (1994), *Intervention, The Use of American Military Force in Post-Cold War World*, A Carnegie Endowment Book: Washington, D.C.

Hall, Raymond L. (ed.) (1979), *Ethnic Autonomy - Comparative Dynamics, The Americans, Europe and the Developing World*, Pergamon Press: New York.

Hannum, Hurst (1990), *Autonomy, Sovereignty, and Self-Determination*, University of Pennsylvania Press: Philadelphia.

Hayden, Robert M. (1992), 'Constitutional Nationalism in the Former Yugoslav Republics', *Slavic Review*, 51, No. 4, pp. 654-73.

Heady, Ferrel (1979), *Public Administration, A Comparative Perspective*, Dekker: New York.

Helsinki Watch, A Division of Human Rights Watch (1992), *War Crimes in Bosnia-Hercegovina*, A Helsinki Watch Report: New York.

Himes, Joseph (1980), *Conflict and Conflict Management*, The University of Georgia Press: Athens, GA.

Hobsbawn, E. J. (1990), *Nations and Nationalism Since 1780.* Cambridge University Press: Cambridge.

Holsti, Kalevi J. (1991), *Peace and War: Armed Conflicts and International Order 1648-1989*, Cambridge University Press: Cambridge.

Hondius, Frits W. (1968), *The Yugoslav Community of Nations*, Mouton, Paris.

Horowitz, Donald L. (1985), *Ethnic Groups in Conflict*, University of California Press: Berkeley.

Horowitz, Donald L. (1990), 'Ethnic Conflict Management for Policymakers', In Montville, Joseph V. (ed.), *Conflict and Peacemaking in Multiethnic Societies*, Lexington Books: Lexington, MA, pp. 115-30.

Horowitz, Donald L. (1991), *A Democratic South Africa? Constitutional Engineering in a Divided Society*, University of California Press: Berkeley.

Horowitz, Donald L. (1994), 'Democracy in Divided Society', In Diamond, Larry and Plattner, Marc F. (eds.), *Nationalism, Ethnic Conflict, and Democracy*, The Johns Hopkins University Press: Baltimore, pp. 35-55.

Horvat, Branko (1969), *Ogled o Jugoslovenskom Drustvu*, Mladost: Zagreb.

Howard, Dick A. E. (ed.) (1993), *Constitution Making in Eastern Europe*, Woodrow Wilson Center Press: Washington, D.C.

Howell, Davbid (ed.) (1993), *Roots of Rural Ethnic Mobilisation, Comparative Studies on Governments and Non-Dominant Ethnic Groups in Europe, 1850-1940*, Dartmouth: England.

Hsu, Shihlien Leonard (1975), *The Political Philosophy of Confucianism*, Curzon Press, London.

Huntington, Samuel P. (1993), 'The Clash of Civilizations,' *Foreign Affairs*, Vol. 72, No.3, pp. 22-49.

Izetbegovic, Alija (1990), *The Islamic Declaration*, BOSNA: Sarajevo.

James, Alan (1986), *Sovereign Statehood, The Basis of International Society*, Allen & Unwin: London.

James, Paul (1992), 'Forms of Abstract 'Community,' From Tribe and Kingdom to Nation and State', *Philosophy of the Social Sciences*, Vol. 22, No. 3, pp. 313-36.

Johnson, Ross A. (1974), *The Future of Yugoslavia*, Rand: Santa Monica, CA.

Joseph, Bernard (1929), *Nationality, Its Nature and Problems*, Yale University Press: New Haven.

Kacowicz, Arie Marcelo (1994), *Peaceful Territorial Change*, University of South Carolina Press: Columbia, SC.

Kahn, Robert L. and Zald, Mayer N. (eds.) (1990), *Organizations and Nation-States, New Perspectives on Conflict and Cooperation*, Oxford: Jossey-Bass Publishers: San Francisco.

Kaiser, David (1994), 'Lessons of the History of Nationalism: Comments', *Theory and Society*, 23, pp. 147-50.

Kaplan, Robert D. (1994), 'The Coming Anarchy', *The Atlantic Monthly*, Vol. 273 No. 2, pp. 44-76.

Kardelj, Edvard (1967), *Neka pitanja skupstinskog i izbornog sistema*, Sedma sila: Beograd.

Kardelj, Edvard (1969), *Raskrsca u razvitku naseg socijalistickog drustva*, Komunist: Beograd.

Kardelj, Edvard (1972), *Tito i Savez Komunista Jugoslavije*, Radnicka stampa: Beograd.

Kedourie, Elie (1993), *Nationalism*, Blackwell: Oxford.

Kellas, James G. (1991), *The Politics of Nationalism and Ethnicity*, St. Martin's Press: New York.

Kenney, George (1995), 'Steering Clear of Balkan Shoals', *The Nation*, January 8, 21-24.

Kis, Theofil I. (1989), *Nationhood, Statehood and the International Status of the Ukrainian SSR/Ukraine*, University of Ottawa Press: Ottawa.

Knith, Jack (1992), *Institutions and Social Conflict*. New York, Cambridge University Press: Cambridge.

Kohn, Hans (1961), *The Idea of Nationalism, A Study in Its Origins and Background*, Macmillan: New York.

Kohn, Hans (1965), *Nationalism, Its Meaning and History*, Van Nostrand: Princeton, NJ.

Kostich, Lazo M. (1981), *Holocaust in the Independent State of Croatia*, Liberty: Chicago.

Krizman, Bogdan (1983), *Ustase i Treci Reich*, Globus: Zagreb.

Kronenberg, Philip and Heaphey, James (1966), *Toward Theory-Building in Comparative Public Administration: A Functional Approach*, CAG (Comparative Administrative Group, American Society for Public Administration) Occasional Paper: Bloomington, IN.

Krooth, Richard and Vladimirovitz, Boris (1993), *Quest for Freedom, The Transformation of Eastern Europe in the 1990s*, McFarland: Jefferson, NC.

Laclau, Ernesto (ed.) (1994), *The Making of Political Identities*, Verso: London.

Lamy, Steven L. (1985), 'Policy Responses to Ethnonationalism: Consociational Engineering in Belgium', Greenwood Press.

Lawrence, Paul R. and Lorsch, Jay W. (1969), *Organization and Environment, Managing Differentiation and Integration*, Irwin: Homewood, IL.

Lijphart, Arend (1977), *Democracy in Plural Societies, A Comparative Exploration*, Yale University Press: New Haven.

Liu, F. T. (1992), *United Nations Peacekeeping and the Non-Use of Force*, International Peace Academy Occasional Paper Series, Lynne Rienner: Boulder, CO.

Lowe, Vaughan and Warbrick, Colin (1994), *The United Nations and the Principles of International Law*, Routledge: London.

Luard, Evan (1982), *A History of the United Nations - Volume 1*, St. Martin's Press: New York.

Malkki, Liisa (1994), 'Citizens of Humanity: Internationalism and the Imagined Community of Nations', *Diaspora*, Vol. 3, No. 1, pp. 41-68.

Maric, Jovan (1985), *Sistem i kriza - Prilog kritickoj analizi ustavnog i politickog sistema Jugoslavie*, Centar za kulturnu djelatnost: Zagreb.

Marius, Richard (1989), *A Short Guide to Writing About History*, Harper Collins: New York.

Marsenic, Dragutin (1990), *Ekonomska Bespuca i Izlazi Socijalizma*, Ekonomika: Beograd.

Mayall James (1990), *Nationalism and International Society*, Cambridge University Press: Cambridge.

McFarlan, Bruce (1988), *Yugoslavia, Politics, Economics and Society*, Pinter: London.

McGarry, John and O'Leary, Brandon (eds.) (1993), *The Politics of Ethnic Conflict Regulations, Case Studies of Protracted Ethnic Conflicts*, Routledge: London.

Menges, Constantine C. (ed.) (1994), *Transitions from Communism in Russia and Eastern Europe*, University Press of America: Lanham, New York.

Mill, John Stuart (1951), *Utilitarianism, Liberty, and Representative Government*, Dutton: New York; originally published in 1861.

Montville, Joseph V. (ed.) (1990), *Conflict and Peacemaking in Multiethnic Societies*, Lexington Books: Lexington, MA.

Morrisson, Christian (ed.) (1993), *Political Feasibility of Adjustment, The Political Dimension of Economic Adjustment*, OECD: Paris.

Moynihan, Daniel Patrick (1993), *Pandaemonium, Ethnicity in International Politics*, Oxford University Press: New York.

Newland, Chester A. (1994), 'Transformational Challenges in Central and Eastern Europe and School of Public Administration', Paper presented at Sixth Annual International Conference on Socio-Economics in Paris.

Niessen, Manfred and Peschar, Jules (eds.) (1982), *International Comparative Research, Problems of Theory, Methodology and Organization in Eastern and Western Europe*, Pergamon Press: Oxford.

Osborne, David and Gaebler, Ted (1993), *Reinventing Government*, Plume: New York.

Pasic, Najdan (1988), 'Discussion', in Djordjevic, Jovan 'The Creation of the 1974 Constitution of the Socialist Federal Republic of Yugoslavia', in Goldwin, Robert A. and Kaufman, Art (eds.) *Constitution Makers on Constitution Making*, American Enterprise Institute: Washington, D.C., pp. 222-4.

Patman, Carole (1970), *Participation and Democratic Theory*, Cambridge University Press: Cambridge.

Pawlowitch, Stevan K. (1988), *The Improbable Survivor, Yugoslavia and its Problems 1918-1988*, Hurst: London.

Pfaff, William (1993), 'Invitation to War', *Foreign Affairs*, Vol. 72, No. 3, pp. 97-109.

Political Report of the Central Committee of the Communist Party of Yugoslavia (1948), Beograd.

Pomerance, Michla (1982), *Self-Determination in Law and Practice, The New Doctrine in the United Nations*, Nijhoff: London.

Porter, Jack Nusan and Taplin, Ruth (1987), *Conflict and Conflict Resolution, A Sociological Introduction with Updated Bibliography and Theory Section*, University Press of America: Lanham, New York.

Ra'anan, Uri (1990), 'The Nation-State Fallacy', in Montville, Joseph V., *Conflict and Peacemaking in Multiethnic Societies*, Lexington Books: Lexington, MA., pp. 5-20.

Ramet, Sabrina P. (1992), *Nationalism and Federalism in Yugoslavia, 1962-1991*, Indiana University Press: Bloomington, IN.

Rae, Douglas W. and Taylor, Michael (1970), *The Analysis of Political Cleavages*, Yale University Press: New Haven.

Report of the European Community Arbitration Committee (1992), *Yugoslav Survey*, No. 1.

Report on the Historical Background of the Civil War in the Former Yugoslavia (1994), United Nations Office in Geneva, prepared by United Nations Commission of Experts, Security Council Resolution 780 (1992) - Chairman Prof. M. Cherif Bassiouni.

Rex, John (1981), *Social Conflict, A Conceptual and Theoretical Analysis*, Longman: London.

Riggs, Fred W. (ed.) (1985), *Ethnicity: INTERCOCTA Glossary, Concepts and Terms Used in Ethnicity Research*, Pilot edition, Department of Political Science, University of Hawaii: Honolulu.

Riggs, Fred W. (1994), 'Ethnonational Rebellions and Viable Constitutionalism', Draft paper for IPSA Congress, Berlin.

Rosenau, James N. (1992), *The United Nations in a Turbulent World*, Rienner: Boulder, CO.

Rupesinge (1992), in *Peace and Conflict Issues After the Cold War*, UNESCO Studies of Peace and Conflict, UNESCO: Paris.

Said, Abdul and Simmons, Luiz R. (eds.) (1976), *Ethnicity in an International Context*. New, Transaction Books: Brunswick, NJ.

Sandole, Dennis J. D. and van der Merwe, Hugo (eds.) (1993), *Conflict Resolution Theory and Practice*, Manchester University Press: Manchester.

Schlesinger, Jr., Arthur M. (1992), *The Disuniting of America*, Norton: New York.

Scott, Richard W. (1981), *Organizations, Rational, Natural, and Open Systems*, Prentice-Hall: Englewood Cliffs, NJ.

Seroka, Jim and Pavlovic, Vukasin (eds.) (1992), *The Tragedy of Yugoslavia, The Failure of Democratic Transformation*, Sharpe: Armonk, New York.

Seton-Watson, Hugh (1977), *Nations and States, An Enquiry in the Origins of Nations and the Politics of Nationalism*, Westview Press: Boulder, CO.

Shafer, Boyd C. (1966), *Nationalism: Interpretations and Interpreters*, Waverly Press: Baltimore, MD.

Sharpe, L. J. (ed.) (1979), *Decentralist Trends in Western Democracies*, Sage Publications: Beverly Hills.

Shibutani, Tamotsu and Kwan, Kian M. (1965), *Ethnic Stratification*, MacMillan: New York.

Shoemaker, Wesley M. (1993), *Russia, Eurasian States and Eastern Europe 1993*, Stryker-Post: Washington, D. C.

Silber, Laura and Little, Allan (1995), *The Death of Yugoslavia*, Penguin Books: London.

Smerdel, Branko, (1994), 'Violent Confrontations and the Political Theory of a Compound Republic: Croatian Experience', Paper presented at the Workshop in Political Theory and Political Analysis, Indiana University, Bloomington.

Smith, Anthony D. (1981), *The Ethnic Revival*, Cambridge University Press: Cambridge.

Smith, Anthony D. (1983), *Theories of Nationalism*, Holmes & Meier: New York.

Smith, Anthony D. (1991), *National Identity*, University of Nevada Press: Reno.

Smith, Mark (1993), *Pax Russica: Russia's Monroe Doctrine*, Royal United Services Institute for Defense Studies: London.

Smith, Paul (ed.) in collaboration with Koufa, Kalliopi and Suppan, Arnold, (1991), *Ethnic Groups in International Relations*, Comparative Studies on Governments and Non-dominant Ethnic Groups in Europe, 1850-1940, Volume V, New York University Press: New York.

Spanier, John (1993), *Games Nations Play*, Congressional Quarterly: Washington, D. C.

Stanovcic, Vojislav (1988), 'Discussion', in Djordjevic, Jovan. 'The Creation of the 1974 Constitution of the Socialist Federal Republic of Yugoslavia - Discussion', in Goldwin, Robert A. and Kaufman, Art (eds.), *Constitution Makers on Constitution Making*, American Enterprise Institute: Washington, D.C., pp. 224-6.

Stanovnik, Janez (1983), *Medjunarodni privredni sistem - Od dominacije ka ravnopravnosti*, Izdavacki centar Komunist: Beograd.

Staudt, Kathleen (1991), *Managing Development, State, Society, and International Contexts*, SAGE Publications: Newbury Park, CA.

Stranjakovic, Dragoslav (1991), *Najveci Zlocini Sadasnjice*, Decije Novine Jedinstvo: Gornji Milanovac.

Strugar, Vlado (1991), *Srbi, Hrvati, Slovenci i Treca Jugoslavija*, Strucna Knjiga: Beograd.

Symmones-Symonolewicz, Konstantin (1986), *Modern Nationalism: Towards a Consensus in Theory*, Czas: New York.

Taylor, Charles W. (1992), *A World 2010, A New Order of Nations*, Strategic Studies Institute, United States Army War College: Carlisle Barracks, Pennsylvania.

Thomas, Theodore H. and Brinkerhoff, Deric W. (1978), *Devolutionary Strategies for Development Administration*, SICA (Section on International and Comparative Administration, American Society for Public Administration) Occasional Paper: Washington, D. C.

Thompson, Kenneth W. (1994), *Fathers of International Thought, The Legacy of Political Theory*, Louisiana State University Press: Baton Rouge.

Tilly, Charles (1990), *Coercion, Capital, and European States, AD 990-1990*, Blackwell: Cambridge, MA.

Tilly, Charles (1994), 'States and Nationalism in Europe 1492-1992', *Theory and Society*, 23, pp. 131-46.

Tishkov, Valery A. (1993), 'Nationalities and Conflicting Ethnicity in Post-Communist Russia', Working Paper Series, Conflict Management Group: Cambridge, MA.

Tito, Josip Broz (1948), *Nationalismus and Internationalismus*, Belgrade.

Tito, Josip Broz (1970), *Tito govori. Split, Zadar, Sisak, Brestovacka Banja, Bor, Zagreb, Beograd, Sabac, Zrenjanin, Kikinda, Sarajevo*, Komunist: Beograd.

Tivey, Leonard (1981), *The Nation-State, the Formation of Modern Politics*, St. Martin's Press: New York.

Toulmin, Stephen (1990), *Cosmopolis, The Hidden Agenda of Modernity*, Free Press: New York.

Treverton, Gregory F. (ed.) (1992), *The Shape of the New Europe*, Council on Foreign Relations Press: New York.

Trifunovska, Snezana (ed.) (1994), *Yugoslavia Through Documents - From Its Creation to Its Dissolution*, Martinus Nijhoff Publishers: Dordrecht.

Tudjman, Franjo (1981), *Nationalism in Contemporary Europe*, East European Monographs: Boulder, CO.

Tummala, Krishna K. (ed.) (1982), *Administrative Systems Abroad*, University Press of America: Lanham.

Twining, William (ed.) (1991), *Issues of Self-Determination*, Aberdeen University Press: Aberdeen.

UNESCO Studies on Peace and Conflict (1992), *Peace and Conflict Issues After the Cold War*, UNESCO: Paris.

United Nations, (1991), *Administrative Modernization in Central and Eastern European Countries*, A Case Study on Decentralization and Public Administration - Report of an Expert Working Group Meeting in Budapest, Hungary.

Vatikiotis, P.J. (1987), *Islam and the State*, Croom Helm: London.

Veselica, Marko (1980), *The Croatian National Question-Yugoslavia's Achilles' Heel*, United Publishers: London.

Vincent, Andrew (1987), *Theories of the State*, Blackwell: Oxford.

Waldo, Dwight (1948), *The Administrative State*, Ronald Press: New York.

Waltz, Kenneth N. (1959), *Man, the State and War*, Columbia University Press: New York.

Weatherford, Roy (1993), *World Peace and the Human Family*, Routledge: London.

Weber, Max (1958), *Essays in Sociology*, Translated and edited by H. H. Gereth and C. Wright Mills, a Galaxy Book, Oxford University Press: New York.

Weber, Max (1966), *The Theory of Social and Economic Organizations*, Translated by A.M. Henderson and Talcott Parsons, edited by Talcott Parsons, Free Press: New York.

White, N. D. (1993), *Keeping the Peace, The United Nations and the Maintenance of International Peace and Security*, Manchester University Press: Manchester.

Whitefield, Stephen (ed.) (1993), *The New Institutional Architecture of Eastern Europe*, St. Martin's Press: New York.

Williams, Colin H. (ed.) (1982), *National Separatism*, University of British Columbia Press: Vancouver.

Williams, Colin H. (1994), *Called Unto Liberty, On Language and Nationalism*, Multilingual Matters: Clevedon.

Woodward, Susan L. (1995), *Balkan Tragedy, Chaos and Dissolution After the Cold War*, Brookings Institution: Washington, D.C.

Wrong, Denis H. (1994), *The Problem of Order, What Unites and Divides Society*, Free Press: New York.

Young, Crawford (ed.) (1993), *The Rising Tide of Cultural Pluralism, The Nation-State at Bay*, University of Wisconsin Press: Madison.

Young, Crawford (1994), 'Ethnic Diversity and Public Policy: An Overview', United Nations Research Institute for Social Development, World Summit for Social Development Draft Occasional Paper: Geneva.

Zametica, John (1992), *The Yugoslav Conflict*, Adelphi Paper 270, International Institute for Strategic Studies: London.

Zarkovic Bookman, Milica (1994), *Economic Decline and Nationalism in the Balkans*, St. Martin's Press: New York.

Zarkovic Bookman, Milica (1992), *The Economics of Secession*, St. Martin's Press: New York.

Zimmemann, Warren (1995), 'The Last Ambassador, A Memoir of the Collapse of Yugoslavia', *Foreign Affairs*, Vol. 74, No. 2, pp. 1-20.

Zivkovic Dragisa (ed.) (1983), *Zasnivanje nacionalne kritike*, Matica Srpska: Novi Sad.